# Techniques for the Analysis of Human Movement

# Techniques for the Analysis of Human Movement

by

D.W. GRIEVE, D.I. MILLER, D. MITCHELSON, J.P. PAUL & A.J. SMITH.

PRINCETON BOOK COMPANY, PUBLISHERS
Princeton, New Jersey 1976

Standard Book Number 86019 006 4

Princeton Book Company Edition 1976

Printed in the United States of America

# Contents

# Preface

The emergence of Human Movement as a field of study (Brooke & Whiting (1973) has inevitably led to the development of more and more sophisticated techniques for the evaluation of movement following on the kind of questions for which answers are sought. The more such developments are concerned with explanation rather than simple description, the more sophisticated and specific the instrumentation and methods tend to become. At the same time, the broad spectrum of questions about human movement which are the concern of the worker in this field, necessitates knowledge and experience of a wide range of techniques which may be used in isolation or in conjunction with one another.

In everyday social interaction situations, we make decisions based on qualitative and quantitative analyses of movement. Attempts have been made to systematise such observational procedures with a view to using movement behaviour as an indicator of stable personality traits (Vernon & Allport 1933; Lamb 1965; North 1973) or as indicators of psychopathology (Breur & Freud 1968; Kanner 1944; Nathan 1967) but the subjective nature of such approaches has limited their development being constrained as they are by subjective observation of transient movement patterns. This is not to deny the usefulness of such techniques but to note that such methods are inherently less conducive to the more objective, detailed analyses of a descriptive, explanatory or prognostic nature with which this book is concerned.

The evaluation of certain sporting events, for example, is dependent on observational techniques—usually by trained observers—and such techniques must extend back a considerable way in man's history. Only when questions began to be asked about the significance of particular kinds of movement and ways in which movement behaviour might be influenced was progress made in both instrumentation and methodology in an attempt to provide some of the answers. No doubt a reciprocal influence is operating here—the search for answers leading to the development of appropriate instrumentation and methodology and the information so obtained leading to more fundamental questions being asked.

Some of the impetus for the development of the study of human movement occurred as early as the beginning of the nineteenth century (Weber & Weber

1894) when attempts were made not only to observe movement on a more objective basis, but to utilise measurement techniques. These early workers were considerably handicapped by their instrumentation and technical expertise, in particular their inability to deal adequately with rapidly changing spatio-temporal situations with limited technological expertise. Perhaps the first major breakthrough in the scientific analysis of human movement followed on the development of instantaneous photography and cinephotography. The scientific and technological climate of the time is summarised by Bernstein (1967):

> It was at just this time (*1860's*) that energetic attempts to decipher the physiological mechanisms of human motor skills were begun; the end of the 19th century is marked in our field by such outstanding studies as those of Muybridge in the United States, Marey in France, and Braune and Fischer in Germany. The methodological innovations of the first two authors form the basis of later developments in cinematography; the last two authors laid the foundations of rigourously scientific quantitative investigation of movements with the help of photography.

The science of human movements (as he called it) was already well recognised by Bernstein.

Inevitably, the exploitation of photographic techniques in the context of human movement study led to an increase in knowledge, the posing of more searching questions and recognition of the limitations of the methodology. Further developments both in instrumentation and methodology have followed fairly rapidly, designed to handle these kinds of problem. In so doing, previous techniques for the analysis of human movement are not being displaced but rather it is being said that if you wish to work at this particular level of analysis or answer these particular questions then this instrumentation and methodology is appropriate. As a result, we have at the present time a variety of techniques and methods for the analysis of human movement which contribute some of the picture, but not all. It is likely in consequence that a combination of methods will be necessary for any comprehensive appraisal of even simple movements.

Photographic techniques have developed considerably since the pioneering studies already referred to. Their biggest impact was perhaps the opportunity to 'capture' complex movement sequences and make them available for detailed analysis at a later date. Here a differentiation is being made between a recording procedure and an analytic technique. It is not sufficient to record movement, detailed measurements must be made from film and inferences drawn from their analysis. There are thus two major sources of error and two major problems of reliability and validity. Additional advantages of photographic techniques are the remoteness of the instrumentation from the subject—no interference from electrodes and wire leads (unless being used in conjunction with other methods)—and the fact that the subject may be filmed without his knowledge thus improving the validity of the measurements as criteria of actual performance and obviating influences such as manifest themselves in the Hawthorne effect (Roethlisberger & Dickson 1939). This is not to deny that there are problems in the use of cinephotographic techniques. Characteristic lack of definition, inaccurate location of points on the body, analysis time, impossibility of monitoring the film record during movement have all been raised as criticisms of this form of evaluation. In fact, much of the development of cinephotographic techniques for the study of human movement has been concerned with minimising error from these kinds of situation. In so doing, not only has the instrumentation been refined, but techniques for analysing data from the film and making inferences from such data have been elaborated. In Section 1, Dr. Smith discusses the use of photographic techniques with particular attention to methods which minimise the possibilities of wrong inferences being drawn but at the same time to retain the obvious advantages of such a technique for the recording and analysis of external parameters of movement.

A more recent analytical development which does not require the use of transducers which may hinder movement is that which utilises polarised light gonimoetry (Polgon). In addition, this method has the advantage that it can produce useful recordings of movement in real time. This in itself can be an important factor in the choice of any analytical methods. In particular, the Polgon method obviates the extended time which is necessary to transcribe data from cine films. In section 2, Mr. Mitchelson describes a Polgon method which he has been developing over a period of years at the Loughborough University of Technology and suggests ways in which this kind of technique might be utilised in the analysis of human movement.

In many studies of human movement, one is less concerned with descriptions of particular movement patterns in situ and more with questions about what would happen *if*!

*If* the take-off angle were increased in the long jump
*If* more force were applied to the discus
*If* the angular velocity of the recovery leg in running was increased etc.

While it would be possible—although very time consuming—to carry out such adjustments in situ analysing each change and then making strategy decisions, there is an obvious advantage in manipulating parameters of this nature freely in order to establish optimal strategies before prescribing training procedures. The computer provides a very useful way of mathematically representing a system and studying the influence of a single variable or combination of variables on the operation of the system as a whole. Simulation methods of this kind are relatively novel. Professor Miller who contributes Section 3 on Computer Simulation has been particularly active in developing this kind of analytic procedure in relation to sporting activities.

Some of the difficulties implicit in the above techniques, particularly where the elevation of the forces operating around any joint complex is the immediate concern of the investigator, have led to the development of a whole range of instrumentation concerned with force measurement—ranging from simple hand dynamometers to elaborate force-platforms designed to record forces operating in three dimensions. The problem with kinetic movement studies based on cine or goniometric techniques is that the required force information cannot be objectively inferred from these techniques alone. It is necessary to measure such forces by other forms of instrumentation and to use these in conjunction with the measurement of limb segment configuration. Techniques for the assessment of force resulting from muscle action are discussed by Professor Paul in Section 4.

As one moves from descriptive studies into deeper levels of explanation of observed external movement characteristics it is necessary to utilise a whole range of additional techniques. Thus, in attributing the forces and torques acting about chosen sections of the body during movement which have been derived from photographic analysis, accelerometry, external force measurement and dynamic anthropometry, to specific structures within the section, it is necessary to utilise techniques like radiography, ultrasonics, manometry and electromyography. Perhaps the most important of these in the present context is electromyography. In Section 5 of this book, Dr. Grieve discusses these kinds of technique with special emphasis on the development of electromyography as an analytic procedure in the study of human movement.

This book is aimed at all students of human movement. It will probably find its greatest application with those more scientifically biased operating at the undergraduate level. However, the way in which it is presented should not put it beyond the scope of the intelligent sixth former concerned with applying his scientific knowledge in a field which is the immediate concern of everyone.

Leeds
May 1974

H.T.A. Whiting
Series Editor

**References**

BERNSTEIN, N. (1967). *The Coordination and Regulation of Movements.* London: Pergamon.

BROOKE, J.D. & WHITING, H.T.A. (Eds.) (1973). *Human Movement*—a field of study. London: Henry Kimpton.

KANNER, L. (1944). Early infantile autism. *J. Paediatrics,* **25,** 211-217.

LAMB, W. (1965). *Posture and Gesture:* an introduction to the study of physical behaviour. London: Duckworth.

NATHAN, P.E. (1967). *Cues, Decisions and Diagnoses.* New York: Academic Press.

NORTH, M. (1973). *Personality Assessment through Movement.* London: MacDonald & Evans.

ROETHLISBERGER, F.J. & DICKSON, W.J. (1939). *Management and the Worker.* Cambridge: Harvard University Press.

VERNON, P.E. & ALLPORT, G. (1933). *Studies in Expressive Movement.* London: MacMillan.

# 1

# PHOTOGRAPHIC ANALYSIS OF MOVEMENT

# PHOTOGRAPHIC ANALYSIS OF MOVEMENT

by A.J. SMITH.

## 1. Introduction

Cine filming may be regarded as a technique for recording and storing information on human activity. As an experimental method it is versatile and simple, and the film may be taken with little or no restriction on the performer's range of movement. The setting may be a laboratory, studio, swimming pool, sports field or athletics track. Information recorded on the film is permanent and detailed, and the filmed activity may be examined in slow motion or 'frozen' at any point. Further, cameras and projection equipment, together with film processing techniques are highly developed and demand no great expertise in normal use.

The term 'cine analysis' implies that detailed examination of a film record is undertaken, generally to a stage beyond mere slow-motion viewing. Cine analysis proper begins when measurements or drawings of body motions are taken from the film. It may be sufficient for some purposes to plot these data directly in graphical form. Often, however, it is useful to put the measured data through a computational process to provide a more detailed analysis of the motion.

This chapter has been written with two main aims. The first is to provide a survey of the techniques available in modern cine analysis. The second is to guide the reader who proposes to carry out his own filming and analysis. While every cine study will raise its own problems, the matters here discussed should assist in the running of experiments with a minimum of waste in time and film.

The methods described have been used to provide teaching aids, student experimental projects and for more elaborate research. In many instances good results have been achieved with simple equipment and it should not be thought that the more sophisticated devices described herein are essential. The emphasis is on cine film and its analysis*, but the use of a still camera is discussed in the section on 'single-plate methods'.

---

* The Appendix contains the names of suppliers of cine equipment.

## 2. Cine filming as a non-contact recording process

When human movement is to be studied it is important that the subject be allowed as much freedom of action as possible. Many ingenious devices have been developed in attempts to measure some feature of human activity without impeding the performance. For example, small plate plate electrodes with light wire leads are attached to the skin for electromyographic measurements of muscle action; a mouth-and-nose mask is used in physiological assessments of oxygen consumption; accelerometers and angle-indicating instruments (elgons) are strapped to the limbs and connected by wiring to a recording system. Recent electronic advances are making such wire connections obsolescent and instead, the signals from electromyographic sensors, heart-rate monitors, accelerometers and other transducers may be relayed by matchbox-sized transmitter units attached to the performer's body.

Such refined instrumentation allows the subject fairly unrestricted movement, but cine filming stands apart as a technique for movement analysis. It is unique in that no apparatus need be attached to the performer, and indeed the filming process may go on without his knowledge. Cine filming is, in effect, a non-contact, remote process of recording data which may later be analysed at leisure. The value of such a process for movement study is fairly obvious, but the further possibility of remote operation of a camera without the subject's knowledge is also important. Any method of movement study which puts the subject in an unusual situation and makes him feel that he is being treated as an experimental animal may affect his performance in subtle but important ways. Such mental interference with a movement pattern will be particularly important in skilled actions. The mere knowledge that one is being filmed is an impediment to natural motion. Most people have had such an experience even when a still camera is being used. The interference with a skilled movement pattern when a subject is festooned with electrodes and wire leads can not be clearly ascertained. Experimenters have to hope that the performer will get used to the idea and gradually revert to normal activity after a period of acclimatisation. The more this hope can be converted into reality by minimising instrumentation and allowing the subject to proceed under normal conditions, the better will be the chances of measuring what really goes on in skilled motion patterns.

Cine filming, then, appears to offer a means of recording information on a human action in a manner which has advantages over practically any other technique at present employed. It is our task to discuss how such information can be used and to recognise the problems involved. It should be noted that cine methods cannot be expected to *replace* such techniques as electromyography or expired air analysis, but they may in many instances offer a valuable alternative. For example, it is unlikely that we shall ever be able to use any experimental method other than filming during Olympic performances. It is therefore important that we explore the possibilities of analysing that film to the full.

## 3. The uses of cine film in movement studies

The most direct use of cine film is slow-motion viewing. Slow-motion film of sporting events allows the eye to respond to detail which could otherwise be misinterpreted or missed completely. In a subjective fashion the viewer can abstract more information than is possible at normal projection speed. This is, however, an elementary use of cine, and assessment of the filmed performance is left to the 'eye' and judgement of the viewer. If cine is to be used as an experimental method, the information stored on the film must be analysed by more precise means.

The first step in moving from subjective judgement of a film to objective analysis is the measurement of movements of various parts of the body. These *displacement* measurements are often made by projecting the film of the activity, one frame at a time, on to a large screen and using ruler, dividers and protractor to read off the required distances and angles. A knowledge of the scale of the projected picture and the speed at which the film was run allows the measured data to be tabulated as a set of distance-time and angle-time relationships. Displacement-time graphs plotted from these tables represent features of the motion pattern which are undetectable by slow-motion viewing and condense much information into an assimilable form.

Other types of displacement representation have been proposed. Grieve's angle-angle loci (section 4) compress the characteristics of the walking stride into two or three informative diagrams. 'Stick-man' tracings of successive body positions are also useful in bringing out the essentials of the motion sequence.

Analysis may be taken further by calculation of velocities, accelerations and other dynamic quantities from the displacement data. Several lines may be followed, depending on the ultimate aim of the analysis. Suffice it here to give some examples of types of study in which cine analysis has been usefully applied. The topics are arranged roughly in order of increasing computational complexity:-

The angular motion of the thigh, shank and foot in locomotion. (Bresler & Frankel, 1950).
The motion of the centre of gravity of the human body in the high jump. (Cooper, 1967).
The aerial rotations of divers and gymnasts. (Lanoue, 1940).
The forces produced by the feet on the ground in a jumping action. (Smith, 1972).
The forces within the body at the knee and hip joints during walking. (Paul, 1965).

The term 'cine analysis' refers to the whole process of taking film of a movement, reading off the displacement data and carrying out the necessary calculations. Before looking at each stage in more detail, it is important to recognise that practical difficulties will arise in most cine studies.

## 4. Some problems in cine analysis

Against the obvious advantages of cine as a remote non-contact recording process there are some drawbacks, which lie mainly in the inherent inaccuracies of measurement and in the sheer volume of computation involved.

### (a) Sources of error

There are six common problems:-
1. Graininess and lack of definition of the film lead to inaccurate location of points on the body of the subject.
2. Markers placed on the body may shift with muscular contraction and stretching of the skin, although they are assumed to indicate bony hinge points beneath the skin.
3. Often assumptions have to be made concerning the weights and dimensions of parts or segments of the body, and it is difficult to check how accurately they apply to a particular subject.
4. The motion viewed by the camera should ideally be in a plane perpendicular to the camera axis. In reality human motion will involve some movement of the limbs out of this ideal plane, even if the general course of the action is at right angles to the line of view. These movements toward and away from the camera lead to changes in the apparent dimensions of parts of the body. The term 'parallax' is sometimes used to refer to this type of error. Without three-dimensional filming (q.v.) it is impossible to make proper correction for the error, but an approximate correction may be written into the computational procedure so that all displacements taken from the film are multiplied by an appropriate factor (Plagenhoef, 1971). In practice a large camera-to-subject distance can reduce this correction factor to a very small value.
5. The data obtained by direct measurement on the film are somewhat distorted by the above inaccuracies. In the terminology of communication engineering 'the signal is contaminated by noise'. Some form of 'noise' removal or smoothing of the data is usually necessary and this will interfere with the genuine information contained in the 'signal'.
6. The final object is usually the calculation of specific results from the film measurements. Velocities, accelerations or forces may be needed and the process of calculation will probably involve further error in the application of approximate methods.

It may at first appear that the combination of these inaccuracies will make the final results suspect, but it is possible to make good sense of cine analysis despite errors in the process. The prospective user should be aware that these problems exist and that techniques are available to counteract some of them.

### (b) Data handling

If the cine record is to be used only as a source of displacement diagrams and 'stick-man' patterns, the quantity of data to be handled is relatively modest. Calculations may be unnecessary and, at most, it may be desirable to incorporate a linear scale factor relating the projected film to its full-size counterpart, and a time-scale based on the running speed of the film.

There is a marked increase in the volume of numerical work if calculations of velocity, acceleration or force are to be made, and if other mechanical quantities are to be derived. At the same time errors in the cine data begin to be more troublesome. Any computational scheme must take account of these factors.

A desk calculator must be regarded as essential to any worthwhile cine analysis. The amount of numerical work may be a daunting prospect, but systematic planning in tabular form clarifies the process and helps to break it into manageable sections. Periodic column and row total checks should be used to eliminate computational slips. Desk machines having programming facilities and paper tape or card input offer some relief in repetitive calculations, but the simpler versions are more easily understood and operated by the beginner and are adequate for pilot studies.

For long runs of film and repeated analyses there is a clear case for putting the work on to a digital computer. A suitable programme must be written, for it is unlikely that standard library programmes for the computer will be of immediate value in cine applications. Some biomechanical papers (Chaffin, 1969; Plagenhoef, 1971) deal with programmes for particular types of motion analysis, but it is important, if a computer programme is to be adopted, that it be tested carefully to ensure that the results are reliable in the new application. On the other hand, if a new programme is to be written it is advisable to carry out full sample calculations 'by hand' so that the mathematical procedures and their logical ordering are properly understood. Programme testing and correction is time consuming and the move from desk work to the computer should be planned carefully.

### 5. The conduct of a cine study

### (a) Cine cameras

Space does not allow more than a brief review of the characteristics of some cine cameras which are suitable for human movement studies. Although 8 mm cameras might be used for preliminary work, it is usual to employ 16 mm cameras for most scientific purposes. A range of good cameras is available in this category.

For small amounts of film it is hardly worth buying a camera. Many colleges and similar establishments possess 16 mm cameras for artistic or scientific work and, as cameras are often under-employed the possibility of borrowing one should be considered.

The terms 'camera speed', 'film speed' and 'framing rate' generally have the same meaning and in the following discussion are used interchangeably. As a guide, it is seldom worth taking film of human activity at more than 300 frames per second. Detailed study of impact situations may call for higher speed filming because impacts, and the events following from them, take place in a very few frames, even at 300 per second. Thus, the choice of camera speed is to some extent governed by the type of information required from the film. In practice it will be found that a great deal of useful biomechanical study can be economically and accurately carried out at film speeds between 32 and 100 frames per second.

The higher framing rates are wasteful of film. For example, it may be possible to film four or five standing long jumps on 100 ft of film at 300 frames per second; but at 1000 frames per second only one jump will be recorded because a considerable length of film is run through the camera as it builds up to full speed and slows down at the end of the run.

Ideally the camera will have a range of speed settings and will provide some form of built-in indication of the film speed. It is unwise to rely too much on the nominal speed of a camera unless a recent calibration has been made. If a stroboscope is available the camera speed may be measured accurately by 'strobing' the shutter while the camera is running.* It is necessary to run film through the camera during this process and, rather than waste new film, a dummy run with an exposed length may be made.

The timing-light device incorporated in more expensive cameras, flashes at mains frequency, which should be steady at 50 cycles per second. Each flash produces a short streak at the edge of the film, and it is a simple matter to check the film speed by counting a number of flash marks and the corresponding frames on the exposed film. Mains frequency itself will usually be a precise 50 cycles per second, but occasional fluctuations occur and an independent check may be made with a stroboscope having a mains frequency input socket.

Cameras with pin-register framing mechanisms ensure that each frame is precisely positioned and stationary as the shutter opens and the picture is taken. The traditional framing system relies on friction alone to position the film and

*I am indebted to my colleague Eric Daniels and to representatives of Dawe Instruments Ltd. for the idea of shutter 'strobing'.

there is a danger of slip and imprecise frame location, especially at higher speeds. It is worth noting here that some film analyser projectors use pin-register positioning and they can only yield their best results if the film is taken with a pin-register camera.

## (b) The experimental area

If the activity is to be carried out under 'laboratory' conditions then prior preparation of the area may be undertaken. The essential requirements are fairly simple and it should also be possible to provide them when filming outside the laboratory. The following facilities are needed:-

a black backcloth
a distance scale
horizontal and vertical reference lines
a timing device, if the framing rate is in doubt.

### Backcloth

Large rolls of matt black paper are available from photographic suppliers and provide a backing which may be set up and removed within minutes. Black curtain is more durable and, if provided with hooks, rings or a supporting rail, is also quickly positioned. Some cotton and man-made fibre materials exhibit an unpleasant reflective sheen under the intense lighting required for filming. A rough black material is preferable and will cut out specular reflection.

### Distance Scale

The distance scale may be a straight bar with equal distances marked clearly on it. Black on white will be necessary if accurate scaling is to be made during film analysis. Fairly large divisions, feet, half-metres or some other suitable unit, are adequate for studies on the whole human body. All that is necessary is that the scaling should establish a relationship between a true length and its apparent length as seen on the projected film. It is important to place the distance scale in the plane of the motion. If the scale will impede the performer, a few frames of film may be run at the start of the experiment to record the distance scale alone, and subsequent filming may be carried out with the scale removed and the working area completely clear. A more elaborate reference may be preferred. Some experimenters use a square grid of fine white lines on a black backboard or a set of horizontal and vertical strings on a rectangular frame. Such scales cannot, of course, be left in the plane of movement, and if they are placed behind the performer a correction will be necessary to allow for the 'depth' error. As with the bar scale, the grid may be filmed on the first few frames and then removed. In case the film is to be used some time after the date of filming it is worth inscribing the true length of a unit on the distance scale so that no confusion can arise.

### Reference Axes

A vertical reference is easily provided by hanging a plumbline of white cord well behind the plane of activity. The horizontal reference may be a distinct line on the floor. It must be perpendicular to both the plumbline and the line cf view of the camera. As well as providing a means of correct orientation of the projected film frames, the vertical and horizontal references are important as datum lines on the picture from which the co-ordinates of points on the body will be measured. They should therefore be visible to the camera throughout the filming process.

### Timing

If the cine camera to be used for motion filming does not possess a timing light system (see 5 (a)), the experimenter has a choice of at least four methods to determine the frame rate of his film:-

1. assume that the nominal frame rate of the camera is correct
2. calibrate the camera just before the experiment by shutter 'strobing' (5 (a))
3. place a clock or other timing device in the camera's field of view
4. superimpose a view of a timing device on the main picture by an optical 'beam-splitting' technique.

The first of these possibilities is satisfactory only if the camera has recently been calibrated or if no accurate work is to be done with the film. The second has already been described and is recommended if a stroboscope is available.

The third has the advantage of providing a permanent record of elapsed time on the film itself. If an ordinary clock face is employed a 'sweep' second hand may not rotate sufficiently fast for accurate time recording and an adaptation to the gear drive system will be necessary to provide more rapid rotation. Alternatively the 'clock' could be a digital timer in which the glow-lamps may be filmed directly (Miller & Nelson, 1973). Some thought must be given to the siting of the digital display in relation to the main illumination of the film set. It is worth remembering that glass fronted clock faces or display screens are liable to give bright reflections which obscure the clarity of the figures. O'Connell (1968) gives a technique for superimposing a clock dial on the filmed motion. The method may also be used with a digital timer and employs a 'beam-splitter' to combine optically the human action and the timing display on a single picture.

## 6. Preparing the subject

In this discussion we shall consider the preparations necessary for filming a side view of the subject performing a simple activity such as walking, running or a standing jump. Most of the limb and trunk movements will thus be in planes at right angles to the camera axis. Earlier mention in this section of the 'plane of movement' must now be qualified. It cannot be assumed that the human body in side view lies entirely in one plane, although the projected film can only give a two-dimensional representation. However, for many purposes, the side of the body and the limbs nearest the camera may be assumed to move very nearly in a single plane perpendicular to the camera axis. If, in subsequent measurement on the film, only points on the nearer side of the body are considered then the 'plane of movement' becomes a more meaningful concept. It is often justifiable to assume that the limbs furthest from the camera move in the same way as those in the plane of movement from which data are taken.

Biomechanical study of the human body often rests upon the further assumption that the limb joints are simple hinges with clearly defined axes of rotation. This is a simplification which has been found to represent whole-body motions with quite reasonable accuracy. In preparing the subject for cine filming, the main concern is to mark the hinge points on the body as precisely as possible. Black disc markers on the skin or direct marking with a felt pen are the usual methods. Greater contrast may be obtained by whitening the area of skin around the marker. For whole-body motions, markers should be around one-half to one inch diameter. The placing of the discs is fairly simple for the ankle and wrist but problems may be encountered in locating the knee, hip and shoulder joint markers. Certain bony landmarks on the body are used (Plagenhoef, 1971), but anyone making a start on cine analysis is recommended to carry out a few experiments by asking the subject to perform some simple limb flexions and identifying reasonable hinge points by trial and error. A final check against the anatomical landmarks may then be made.

If the skin over the hip joint is to be visible to the camera, the subject will have to wear briefs which are tied up at the side to prevent them obscuring the marker. The elbow and shoulder joints are sometimes not sufficiently well marked by discs, which tend to be rotated out of view during arm flexions. A black band may be used in such cases.

In some studies the interest is not so much in the motion of hinge points as in that of the centres of gravity of the limb segments. While centres of gravity may be calculated from hinge point co-ordinates, there is something to be said for marking the body directly with discs or bands to indicate the centres of gravity themselves. The approximate location of these points may be found in standard biomechanical works (Dyson, 1970; Williams & Lissner, 1966; Miller & Nelson, 1973). The disadvantage in marking centres of gravity on the body is that the markers are mounted on soft tissue somewhere between the hinge points, and are liable to shift appreciably with muscle contraction and stretching of the skin. Sometimes subjects are marked with straight lines joining the hinge points and demarcating the limbs very clearly. The choice of more elaborate marking schemes depends to a large extent on the purpose to which the film is to be put. For demonstration and teaching, multiple marking may well be used to highlight the limb motions, but for bare analysis hinge points alone are sufficient.

It will be obvious that a fully clothed subject wearing, say, a tracksuit marked with distinctive lines, will provide a non-too-accurate film for analytical purposes. The motion of the clothing is likely to be significantly different from that of the body and measured co-ordinates will be unreliable.

## 7. Taking and processing the film

Successful filming generally requires a measure of trial and error with illumination, exposure and film speed. Professional advice is essential if the user is unfamiliar with the camera. Cameras have their own peculiarities and loading of the film can be a considerable problem. If there is a range of interchangeable shutters and lenses unguided experiments with the various combinations can be expensive in time and film. Illumination and exposure setting are also matters of experience. There is no great mystique in cine filming and the beginner will soon learn to produce adequate results if he takes his first lessons from an experienced operator.

A few pointers may be useful since the filming of human motion is somewhat different from the other applications of scientific photography. As to illumination, a single subject performing in an area twenty feet square will need at least 3000 watts of lighting for good results. The lamps should be beamed roughly in the same direction as the camera's line of view but must not obscure the camera's view of the subject. Prior to running the camera it is worth having the subject move around in the area to check the uniformity of the illumination.

The camera should be as far away from the subject as possible to keep 'obliquity' error fairly small, but this requirement will have to be balanced against the focal length, field of view and exposure characteristics of camera and film. The axis of the camera must be at right angles to the plane of motion and aimed at the centre of the area to be covered by the activity. 'Panning', or any other camera movement during filming will add considerable difficulties to subsequent cine analysis and is best avoided.

In addition to the reference scales and lines there may be a need to provide synchronisation of the film with some event in the activity. If, for example, we wish to record the point at which the subject's feet leave the ground in a jump, we may arrange for a pressure switch to open at the instant of take-off and for a lamp in the field of view to be extinguished. It is useful to have such an event marker. The point of take-off is seldom clearly visible on the film because of shadows cast by the feet.

16 mm cine film is usually bought and processed in 100 ft reels. Processing may be stopped at the negative stage or, if required, positive prints may be made. Analysis can be carried out on either positive or negative film, but if the negative is scratched or otherwise damaged during analysis it will be difficult to obtain good positive copies at a later stage.

It is generally possible to have a film 'force-developed' if it is under-exposed. High-speed filming with inadequate lighting often requires this treatment.

Finally it is desirable but not essential to have a permanent film studio to carry out biomechanical studies. Whether filming 'in the field' or in some prepared area, the preparations may be so organised and streamlined that the whole set is assembled or dismantled in about 15 minutes. Two hours should allow prior preparation of the area, filming for well over an hour and complete clearance of the working space at the end of the experiment.

## 8. Projecting the film

### (a) Slide projectors

A first examination of the processed negative or the positive copy may be made with a slide projector having a film-strip attachment. The manufacturers will supply spacing washers to convert the normal 35 mm spools to 16 mm, but it is quite easy to arrange suitable guides and run the 16 mm film on its own spools. Projection by this method shows the full width of the film on the screen, and the timing marks and reference numbers on the edge of the film may be seen clearly. The reference numbers will probably appear every 20 frames and make frame counting easy. The timing marks, if produced by the camera, must also be counted for determination of the frame speed of the film.

The analysis of many activities will involve at most a few hundred frames. At 40 frames per foot the working length can easily be run by hand through the film-strip attachment and frame positioning is not hampered by any driving mechanism. Although better means are available, it is feasible to carry out a full analysis on a slide projector. The main disadvantage will probably be the small projected size of the picture.

## (b) Analysing projectors

The next stage in sophistication is a specialised analysing projector. This device is unlikely to show the timing marks at the edge of the film, but its most important feature is the stationary projection of single frames. A frame counter and push-button feed are usually provided and the projector may be run at steady low speeds for slow-motion viewing. The absence of reference numbers on the projected picture makes it important to mark the frames with some numbering system. A small scratch at the corner of every tenth frame is adequate, but more detailed marking could be done with standard lettering sets.

In the interests of economy one may be tempted to adapt a standard movie projector or build up a suitable lens system. A word of caution may not be out of place. Single frame and slide projectors incorporate a heat filter between the lamp and the film. Without this filter, stationary film will overheat quickly, although the heat is easily dissipated when the film is running normally.

## (c) Screens

The screen for projection will also be the surface on which measurements are taken. A cloth screen is not really suitable even when taut, and for normal forward projection a matt white cleanable panel is best. Alternatively, white cartridge paper taped firmly to a rigid board may be replaced as necessary. The screen must be accurately set at right angles to the projector axis and care must be taken not to disturb the setting during measurement. If the method of scaling suggested earlier is adopted there is no need to project the picture to a particular size; the screen may be at any convenient distance from the projector.

Back-projection calls for a translucent screen behind which the projector is mounted. Ground glass is expensive and unnecessary; an excellent screen can be made by covering plate glass with good quality tracing paper. Sometimes graph tracing paper, marked with rectangular grid lines, may be helpful. One disadvantage of forward projection is that the experimenter tends to block out the area he is attempting to measure. Back-projection eliminates this problem but, on the debit side, it is more difficult to arrange a large back-projection screen (say 3 ft by 4 ft) than to set up a similar screen for forward projection. As a general rule, the larger the projected picture, the more accurate the measurements obtained from it. However, we reach a practical limit in working close to the screen, when grain and lack of definition become troublesome. A 3 ft by 4 ft area is about the largest required for most purposes.

## (d) X-Y Film analysers

These devices further relieve the tedium of reading data from projected frames. The film is shown on a cabinet-mounted back-projection screen by a projector with single-frame feed. Runners at the sides of the screen carry horizontal and vertical sliders with an eyepiece or cursor. When the cursor is located over a particular point on the projected picture, a push-button system can be used to read off the X and Y co-ordinates of the point. A further facility allows the co-ordinates to be punched in standard computer code on paper tape. Angle measurement may also be carried out by rotation of the whole picture on the screen or by the attachment of an accessory to the cursor mounting. Details of these devices are obtainable from the suppliers, some of whom are listed in the Appendix of this section.

## 9. Measurements on the projected film

Once a suitable film is obtained, the measurement to be carried out will depend on the object of the analysis. Some typical aims are set out below:-

1. Shot and hand motion in shot-putting: measure distances along the curved trajectory of the shot during thrust.
2. Angular velocity of the arm in a Karate chop action: measure angles of forearm relative to the vertical reference.
3. Leg action in kicking: measure upper leg, lower leg and foot angles relative to the vertical reference.
4. Motion of whole-body centre of gravity in jumping: measure horizontal and vertical co-ordinates of hinge points (ankle, knee, hip) or of limb centres of gravity, if marked (foot, lower leg etc.) relative to the reference axes.
5. Aerial motion of a highboard diver: measure hinge point co-ordinates and body segment angles relative to the reference axes.

In addition to the recording of such numerical data, it will usually be informative to draw 'stick-man' configurations for each frame and the horizontal and vertical reference lines should be included for correct spatial location.

The measurement of linear co-ordinates does not necessitate the making of marks on the screen. Dividers are useful for picking off the distances, but on a projection of reasonable size many of the dimensions to be measured will lie between 6 and 30 inches. Although large beam compasses are available from drawing office suppliers and could be used as dividers, they are expensive and it will be difficult to find a compass of 30 in. span. The author has made his own beam dividers from a constructional kit. They are rigid, accurate, easily set to a wide range of spans and of negligible cost. Ordinary dividers cover the smaller spans up to about 8 inches.

In a darkened projection room it is useful to have a work table illuminated by a shielded lamp to take the record sheets and a long steel rule. The latter is used to convert divider settings immediately to distances as seen on the projected picture. A wooden rule is less satisfactory because it quickly becomes damaged by the divider needles. When angle measurements are required, a protractor is not easily used in the dark room, and it is better to draw lines on the screen to indicate the required limb positions. Care must be taken to label the lines with their correct frame numbers and to include the horizontal and vertical references. If much overlapping occurs in the drawings, a new paper sheet screen will be needed every few frames. Angle measurements on these drawn lines may be carried out under normal lighting.

Finally, the measurement of the distance scale as it appears on the projected picture must not be forgotten. Once the projector is moved it may be impossible to recreate accurately the projected size from which the original measurements were taken.

It cannot be too strongly emphasised that all measurements should be taken from the reference axes filmed by the camera and appearing in the projected picture. It is sometimes tempting to use the edges of the projection screen as references, but this procedure should be avoided. Appreciable frame jumping, due to camera or projector, makes it inaccurate to regard the projected picture as being in a fixed position on the screen. Even when using an X-Y Analyser it is better to rely on references within the picture than the zero settings on the X and Y sliders.

## 10. Analysis of cine data

We now consider some of the problems encountered in the processing of data from direct measurement on the cine film. The complexity of the problem will depend upon the kind of calculation to be performed and the final result required. As we have seen earlier, it may be sufficient to present the measured quantities graphically, without any intervening calculation. In other cases the interest will be in the whole-body centre of gravity, and the location of hinge points on the body, read from the film, may be used to calculate the trajectory of the centre of gravity.

The analysis is taken to a further stage of difficulty if linear or angular velocities are required. Velocities are obtained by taking the rates-of-change of the displacement co-ordinates. The normal methods of the differential calculus cannot be used because the displacements are not in algebraic form. The tabulated displacement-time data from film measurement must be put through some form of 'numerical differentiation' procedure to produce values of velocity at each frame. The term 'numerical differentiation' covers a range of techniques for dealing with values which are discretly spaced in time, and some smoothing may be incorporated to counter the effects of random errors or 'noise' in the data.

The calculation of accelerations is carried out by taking the differentiation procedure one stage further. The estimation of forces from film analysis depends upon the reliable computation of acceleration values, and in some instances the accelerations are themselves of interest.

As the data go through differentiation processes there is usually a serious magnification of error effects. A velocity curve computed from reasonably accurate displacement data is likely to exhibit some unpleasant bumps which can not be explained as real effects in the movement being analysed. An acceleration curve from the same basic data may be a meaningless succession of violent peaks and troughs. This error magnification problem is always encountered in cine analysis where rates-of-change are to be obtained. Some mathematicians regard numerical differentiation in the presence of such errors to be a dubious procedure and there is certainly no perfect solution. Any successful treatment will incorporate some form of smoothing of the errors before or during differentiation, and it is here that human judgement of the original and the computed results must go hand-in-hand with mathematical procedures. When any smoothing is introduced there is the attendant hazard that real information may be 'rubbed out' together with the error fluctuations which the smoothing is intended to remove.

## 11. An Example of Cine Analysis

### (a) The Use of Smoothing and First Difference Differentiation

We now turn our attention to the practical application of cine analysis to a simple movement. The foregoing description of the difficulties of smoothing and differentiation should not deter us from embarking upon some fairly straight-forward calculations based on cine film measurements. The reason that the problems of cine analysis have been given so much prominence in the earlier part of this chapter is to point out that apparently erratic results may be given a sensible interpretation if the sources of error can be recognised and their effects reduced by well-chosen computational procedures.

The simple example which follows is intended to illustrate methods which are useful for a first approach to this kind of work and which may be carried into the study of quite complex human motions.

Figure 1 shows a succession of arm positions taken from film of a standing long jump just prior to take-off. Consider the angular motion of the arm. The definition of angular displacement is 'the change of angle between a line on the moving body and a fixed reference line'. In the present case, the arm remains straight during the swing, so that the line joining the shoulder to the wrist may be used to represent the moving limb. The fixed reference line is the vertical plumbline in the camera's field of view. Thus we tabulate (Table 1) the

Table 1     (Angles in degrees)

| Frame | (1) Unsmooth-ed angular displace-ments $\theta a$ | (2) Differe-ces from col. (1) $\delta \theta a$ | (3) Smoothed angular displace-ments $\theta b$ | (4) Differences from col. (3) $\delta \theta b$ | (5) smoothed differences $\delta \theta c$ | (6) 5-point second-order differentia-tion * |
|---|---|---|---|---|---|---|
| 1 | 34.5 | | 34.5 | | 8.8 | 10.7 |
| 2 | 48.2 | 13.7 | 50.0 | 15.5 | 21.4 | 21.2 |
| 3 | 76.4 | 28.2 | 77.0 | 27.0 | 31.8 | 30.1 |
| 4 | 112.0 | 35.6 | 113.5 | 36.0 | 38.2 | 36.4 |
| 5 | 151.5 | 39.5 | 153.0 | 39.5 | 40.6 | 39.1 |
| 6 | 193.5 | 42.0 | 194.0 | 41.0 | 40.0 | 37.5 |
| 7 | 225.0 | 31.5 | 232.0 | 38.0 | 34.2 | 32.6 |
| 8 | 258.8 | 33.8 | 261.5 | 29.5 | 25.8 | 25.3 |
| 9 | 283.4 | 24.6 | 282.0 | 20.5 | 17.4 | 17.4 |
| 10 | 295.4 | 12.0 | 295.5 | 13.5 | 9.8 | 10.0 |
| 11 | 302.2 | 6.8 | 302.0 | 6.5 | 3.0 | 3.0 |

*Discussed in 11b, 'Polynomial smoothing-differentiation methods'.

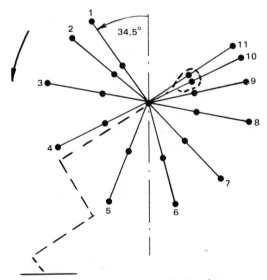

*Fig. 1. Simplified arm-swing pattern during a standing long-jump.*

Note: The body configuration is indicated only approximately. For simplicity the diagram shows the shoulder joint as a fixed centre of rotation although it is, in fact, in motion during the arm swing. It is important to note that such motion of the shoulder hinge-point in no way invalidates the analysis of angular velocity. See the definition of angular motion in 11 a).

successive angular displacements, taking care to measure them all according to the same convention; in this case the angles are measured anticlockwise with the upward vertical as zero. There is no need to try to construct or even conceive of the 'axis about which the rotation occurs'.

Now suppose that the main aim is to estimate the *maximum* angular velocity of the arm during the swing. From the line diagram (Figure 1) the maximum velocity occurs around the middle of the swing. It is tempting to consider only two or three arm angles in this region and ignore the others. However, it will be wiser to take a little more trouble and derive an angular velocity curve for the whole swing. The maximum will then be more clearly defined and the plotting of the complete curve gives some safeguard against stupid errors in calculation.

To express velocities in radians per second—a useful unit—we must convert degrees to radians and divide by the time interval between successive arm positions, 1/22.4 seconds. Some effort can be saved by leaving these conversion constants to be applied at a late stage in the work. Indeed, tabular calculations of any kind are usually speeded up if conversion factors are introduced as late as possible in the process. Thus, in using:-

$$\text{Angular velocity } \omega \quad = \quad \frac{\text{Angular displacement}}{\text{Corresponding time interval}}$$

$$= \quad \frac{\delta\theta}{\delta t}$$

we may rearrange the relationship as:-

$$\omega \text{ (rad/s)} = \frac{\delta\theta \times [\pi \times 22.4]}{180} \quad \left(\text{degrees} \times \frac{\text{radians}}{\text{degrees}} \times \frac{1}{\text{seconds}}\right)$$

In Table 1 the successive differences of the displacements in Column 1 give the $\delta\theta_a$ of column 2, and these latter will be used directly to represent the angular velocity curve, leaving the conversion constant ($\frac{\pi}{180} \times 22.4$) to be inserted later. This difference procedure is rather crude, and a graph of the Column 2 values gives an erratic velocity curve because the whole process is based on displacements contaminated by measurement errors. It is at this stage that some smoothing is desirable, and a more realistic, though lengthier process for obtaining the angular velocities is as follows:-

1. Plot the original displacement points $\theta_a$. (Column 1, Table 1)
2. Draw a smooth curve 'by eye' through these points. (Figure 2)
3. Read from the smooth curve a corrected set of displacements. (Column 3, Table 1)
4. Take successive differences $\delta\theta_b$ from the column 3 smoothed displacements.

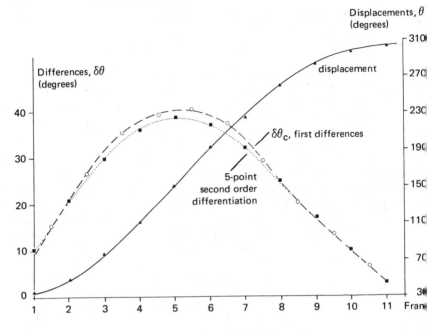

*Fig. 2. Angular Displacements and Angular Velocities*

Note: The curves for first differences and for 5-point differentiation represent angular velocity when the ordinates are
multiplied by the factor $\frac{\pi}{180}$ x 22.4 (11a)

5. Plot the $\delta\theta_b$ as a representation of the angular velocity curve.
6. Draw a smooth curve 'by eye' through the $\delta\theta_b$ points.
7. Read from the latter curve a corrected set of differences $\delta\theta_c$ and use these
   final values to evaluate angular velocities $\omega$ radians per second, introducing
   the conversion constant $\frac{\pi}{180}$ x 22.4 at this stage. (Column 5, Table 1).

It has already been pointed out that any smoothing procedure requires some
experience and judgement on the part of the user for its proper application. In
the operations outlined above, the judging of a 'best-fit' smooth curve calls for
the construction of a curve which passes among, but does not necessarily touch
all the plotted points. Some fluctuations in the plotted values are hereby
removed. It is impossible to give precise rules for the curve fitting procedure, but
the following guides are useful:-

(i) For voluntary human movements, that is, those not involving violent impacts with agencies outside the body, film taken at less than 100 frames per second should present no serious smoothing problems. A smooth displacement curve, for linear or angular motion, will touch many of the plotted displacement points. Perhaps 20–50% of the points will lie off the curve.

(ii) If voluntary movements are recorded at speeds above 100 frames per second, a smoothed displacement curve will probably miss most of the plotted displacement points, rather as a regression line may pass among a cluster of points but touch very few of them. A good rule here is to plot displacement points every 5 or 10 frames, rather than at 1-frame intervals, thereby standing back from the overwhelming detail of the errors and taking a broader view of the general form of the displacement curve. In fact, the data in the present example were taken at 10-frame intervals from a 224 frame per second film.

(iii) If time and patience allow, greater refinement is possible with higher framing speeds. For example, if film at 100 frames per second is to be analysed, two quite separate sets of displacement data may be obtained, one from the even- and one from the odd-numbered frames; each set is equivalent to the taking of a 50 frame per second film. Plotting and curve fitting for the two sets independently of each other leads to two displacement curves which should be similar, both describing the same motion. Careful examination and correction of discrepancies between them should give a final form to the smoothed displacement curve.

The above example deals with the motion during a few frames of the arms only. It will be obvious that cine analysis of the motion of all the body parts, or 'segments' for a large number of frames is a major undertaking in graphical and numerical labour. The value of computer assistance in a comprehensive cine analysis should be clear. Smoothing and differentiating techniques which replace the drawing of graphs by mathematical procedures are well suited to computer applications. Some of these techniques, based on polynomial curve-fitting are described below.

## (b) Polynomial Smoothing-Differentiation Methods.

The 'first-difference' methods of the previous section may be replaced by more sophisticated procedures. Subjective curve-fitting 'by eye' gives way to the mathematical fitting of a polynomial curve to the data points and the subsequent differentiation for velocity and acceleration is based on this polynomial. Techniques of wide applicability are given by Lanczos (1967) in his chapter on Data Analysis. Plagenhoef (1971) uses a rather different type of polynomial method in his computer programme.

The value of a technique based on polynomial curve-fitting is that it can be written into a computer programme, whereas the process of human judgement involved in curve-fitting 'by eye' cannot be described in mathematical terms. Although polynomial methods are mathematically more refined they are not necessarily more accurate than the 'first-difference' procedures previously described. The interested reader is strongly recommended to consult Lanczos (1967), but it is important to keep in mind that the whole process of differentiation of data taken from cine film is subject to errors which are at times quite serious. Moreover, it is not in most cases possible to determine the magnitude of the error involved. As a general rule, the more sudden the fluctuations in the data points the more inaccurate will be the results of differentiation on those data points, but the error problem is not well understood. The formulae of Lanczos are quite widely used in technological computation and the author has attempted an investigation of some features of the differentiation problem for cine data. (Smith 1972).

## 12. Other Methods of Motion Recording

### (a) Three-Dimensional Filming

Until now our discussion has been based upon the assumption that the subject's trunk and limbs move in planes perpendicular to the camera axis. Such two-dimensional motions represent certain body movements with reasonable accuracy, but more complex activities, such as a twisting high-board dive, involve three-dimensional body displacements. In this kind of action, the side of the body initially nearest the camera rotates out of this plane and away from the camera during the dive. For proper analysis of the body motion a single camera is not sufficient. The problem has been tackled by the use of a pair of cameras, say one at the side and one taking a plan view.* The cameras must be synchronised and their axes set to intersect at right angles. Analysis of the double film record calls for geometrical projection techniques familiar in engineering drawing, and the procedures are, of course, much more time consuming than those used in two-dimensional analysis. Alternatively, the mathematical equivalent of the geometrical method may be written into a computational procedure to make the task more manageable.

Miller's work (section 3) on computer simulation in diving, was applied to a three-dimensional problem and two cameras were employed. Another example of the technique is a recent analysis of a full-twist back-somersault (Borms et al 1971). A system of body representation using a link-mechanism model has been

---

*It is also possible to use three cameras simultaneously or a single camera in conjunction with a mirror.

proposed by Plagenhoef (1971) as an extension of his earlier two-dimensional approach (Plagenhoef 1966). This method may provide a useful clarification of the essential characteristics of three-dimensional movement patterns.

The move from two- to three-dimensional film analysis involves a considerable increase in the data to be handled, and this is at present the greatest barrier to progress. If automatic film analysis can be developed (see 13) with the output fed directly to a computer programme, the road will be open to some very interesting work on complex body actions.

## (b) Single-plate Methods

These techniques attempt to record a complete motion pattern on a single picture. A still camera is used in conjunction with special methods of controlling the light admitted to the film. The term-single-plate is used for convenience to refer to any type of film employed in still-cameras—35 mm, polaroid or the bulkier professional plates. Generally, the camera shutter is left open during the filming and one of the following four methods is used to control the exposure:-

## (i) Stroboscopy

The movement takes place in a darkened room. A stroboscope lamp is set to flash at a fixed frequency so that about twenty or thirty flashes will occur during the total time of movement. At each flash an instantaneous, though rather ghostly image of the moving body is recorded by the camera plate. A sequence of about twenty of these images is often adequate to show the motion pattern clearly. Too fast a flash rate causes the images to follow once another too quickly and the final picture will be an undecipherable white cloud. On the other hand, a very slow flash rate may give only two or three images of the whole motion and omit much important detail. The specific value of the flash frequency depends on the rapidity of the movement to be recorded.

As a simple example, a golf-ball, falling freely for one metre will be well recorded at a flash rate of 3000 per minute. The formula $s = \frac{1}{2}gt^2$ shows that the time of fall from rest is about 1/3 second and that approximately 17 images will be obtained.

The translucent quality of stroboscopic pictures is caused by the low intensity of illumination during each flash. It is now possible to run a bank of stroboscopes in synchronisation to enhance illumination but even with this improvement the working area may have to be limited to about 4 m square. With a single stroboscope an area of 1 m square is about the largest for which good results will be obtained.

The picture quality is improved if non-shiny white reflective surfaces predominate on the moving bodies and if the background is the dark volume of a large room. Backcloths reflect the intense beam of a stroboscope to a surprising extent, even when they are made of dull black material. Picture quality is important because stroboscopic work is often more useful for visual aid material than for detailed analysis of movement.

### (ii) Rotating-slit shutter

In some movement studies it is difficult or dangerous for the subject to work in a darkened room with a flashing stroboscope. If he is to work under normal lighting conditions, a single-plate method utilizing a rotating-shutter mechanism is suitable.

The camera shutter itself is left open and a rotating disc is introduced just in front of the lens. The disc is driven at constant speed by a clockwork or electric motor and a radial slit cut into the disc passes before the lens at each revolution. Each passage of the slit serves as a shutter opening to the camera, and the speed of rotation of the disc corresponds to the flash-rate in the stroboscopic method. Ideally, the driving mechanism for the disc will be of variable speed and the shutter frequency may further be varied by the use of discs with two or more equi-spaced slits.

### (iii) Light-streak Photography

If the camera shutter is left open in a dark room and a glowing torch bulb moves across the field of view, its track will be recorded as a well-defined streak. Bulbs attached to the body at the joints and extremities have been used to provide light-streak pictures of human motion. The arcs traced out by these marker bulbs suggest whether the motion is fluent or erratic, and faint impressions of the remainder of the body may be seen on the printed picture.

### (iv) Interrupted-light Photography

The light-streak method is sometimes modified by providing a make-and-break contact in the electrical supply to the lamps. If the contact is opened and closed at a controlled rate by a motor-driven trip device, the marker bulbs on the body glow intermittently. The uninterrupted streak produced by a continuously glowing bulb is now replaced by a chain of short streaks. Thus, the camera records the path of the bulb and also indicates, by the length and spacing of the streaks, the speed and time-scale of the motion.

Much of the appeal of single-plate motion recording lies in the immediate and attractive presentation to the eye of the flow of skilled movement. The best effects are produced by movements which are well-spread across the field of view, but if there is any overlapping in the motion pattern, confusion of the images is inevitable. Thus, normal running will appear well on a single plate, but running on the spot gives rise to a meaningless jumble of superimposed images.

Stroboscopic lamps are commercially produced and it is unlikely that a home-made substitute will suffice. However, the equipment for the other single-plate methods is not generally available from photographic or scientific suppliers and must be built in the laboratory.

A useful survey of single-plate methods may be found in one volume in the published Proceedings of the First International Seminar in Biomechanics (1968). The full title and publisher appear in the references. Examples are given of stroboscopy (Groh & Baumann, pp 23-32), rotating-slit photography (Maier pp 96-101). light-streak pictures (Fetz, pp 45-52) and interrupted-light methods (Gutewort, pp 53-60 and Waterland, pp 178-187).

## 13. Recent Developments in Cine Analysis

### (a) Automatic picture scanning

Completely automatic scanning of each frame of a film sequence appears possible, although it is not an easy task for the scanning device to distinguish between markers on different parts of the body. At present some human intervention in the scanning and reading process seems to be necessary in order to tell the scanner whether it is searching, say, for the knee-joint rather than the ankle-joint marker. The use of television scanning in conjunction with video-tape recording appears to offer an alternative solution, since the projection of a picture on a television screen is associated with a precise horizontal scanning system.

Groh and Baumann (1968) describe a basic system for automatic scanning of cine film. Kasvand et al (1971) give the results of more recent work with a scanning device combined with a digital computer.

### (b) Frequency Analysis of Cine Data

A cine film of an activity is a process of information sampling at regular time intervals, each frame or film records information on the body configuration at a particular instant. As the film speed is increased the rate of sampling, or 'sampling frequency' increases correspondingly. The word 'frequency' has been introduced deliberately, because frequency analysis, well established in certain branches of engineering and physics, is a key to understanding the error problems encountered in cine studies. In a cine record we are provided, in effect, with a steady flow of isolated items of information (the frames of the film) subject to some distortion from various sources. In radio communication the signal received is similarly a steady flow of information contaminated by 'noise', a word describing all forms of unwanted interference of a random nature. The separation of the 'noise' from the real signal may be assisted by electronic filtering devices, and the mathematical study of the effects of filters on signals is well-developed. It is now becoming recognised in biomechanical circles that the principles of noise and signal analysis are applicable to problems encountered in cine studies.

One important technique, that of Fourier Analysis, breaks down a data record into components which are simple sine and cosine forms of various frequencies. A signal contaminated by random 'noise' will often produce fairly large low-frequency components, but the higher frequency terms may be of small magnitude. A result of this sort points to the fact that the higher-frequency terms represent virtually pure 'noise' and that the real information can be described by the low-frequency terms alone. For data from cine film the highest frequency appearing in the Fourier analysis is directly proportional to the film franing-rate, or sampling frequency. Thus, the restriction of real information to a low frequency band and the discarding of the higher frequencies as noise, suggests that the speed of the film used to record the activity was unnecessarily great. If we need only the first few (low-frequency) terms of the Fourier analysis, we could have run the film at a lower speed and still have recorded the information which has real significance. On the other hand, the use of very high frame-rates may add only high-frequency noise terms to the data.

Smoothing of the data may be shown to correspond broadly to the removal of some noise frequencies, but there is in any smoothing process the attendant danger that useful information occurring in this frequency range may also be erased. Judicious application of smoothing techniques is essential.

The exploitation of frequency analysis has not yet been carried far in cine studies of human motion. The reader interested in the fundamentals of these techniques is referred to the informative works of Hamming (1962) and Lanczos (1967). The author has applied Fourier analysis in a human movement study (Smith 1972).

It is probable that the development of automatic picture scanning will be linked with electronic frequency analysis of data measured from the cine film. At present it is possible to display on a television screen the frequency components of a musical note as it is played. A similar continuous monitoring of movement data from a scanned cine film is an intriguing prospect for the future.

## References

*Note:* The Proceedings of the First International Seminar in Biomechanics, Zürich, 1967 have been published (1968) by Karger: Basle and New York, under the title 'Medicine and Sport'. Volume 2 of these Proceedings, which carries the title 'Biomechanics Techniques of Drawings of Movement and Movement Analysis', contains several articles referred to in the text of this chapter, and for simplicity the volume will hereafter be called *Zürich, Vol. 2'.*

BRESLER, B. & FRANKEL, J.P. (1950). The forces and moments in the leg during level walking. *Trans. A.S.M.E.*, **72**, 27-34.

BORMS, J., DUQUET, W. & HEBBELINCK, M., (1971). Biomechanical analysis of the full-twist back-somersault. Third Internation Seminar in Biomechanics, Rome. (to be published by Karger: Basle & New York.)

CHAFFIN, D.B. (1969). A computerized biomechanical model-development of and use in studying gross body actions. *J. Biomech.*, **2**, 429-441.

COOPER, J.M. (1968). Kinesiology of high-jumping. *Zürich, Vol. 2.*, 291-302.

DYSON, G.H.G. (1970). *The Mechanics of Athletics.* London: University Press.

FETZ, F. (1968). Lichtspuraufnahmen. *Zürich, Vol. 2.*, 45-52.

GROH, H. & BAUMANN, W. (1968). Kinematische Bewegungsanalyse. *Zürich, Vol. 2.*, 23-32.

GUTEWORT, W. (1968). Die digitale Erfassung Kinematischen Parameter der Menschlichen Bewegung, *Zürich, Vol. 2.*, 53-60.

HAMMING, R.W. (1962). *Numerical Methods for Scientists and Engineers.* McGraw Hill: New York & London.

KASVAND, T., MILNER, M. & RAPLEY, L.F. (1971). A computer-based system for the analysis of some aspects of human locomotion. I. Mech. E. Conference on Human Locomotor Engineering, University of Sussex, Sept. 1971 (to be published by I. Mech. E., 1 Birdcage Walk, London S.W.1).

LANCZOS, C. (1967). *Applied Analysis.* London: Pitman.

LANOUE, F. (1940). Analysis of the basic factors involved in fancy diving. *Res. Quart.*, **11**, 102-109.

MAIER, I. (1968). Measurement apparatus and analysis methods of the biomotor process of sport movements. *Zürich, Vol. 2.*, 96-101.

MILLER, D. & NELSON, R.C. (1973). *Biomechanics of Sport.* Philadelphia: Lea & Febiger.

O'CONNELL, A.L. (1968). A Simple method of synchronising cinematographic-electromyographic data. *Zürich, Vol. 2.*, 128-131.

PAUL, J.P. (1965). Bioengineering studies of the forces transmitted by joints (ii). in R.M. Kenedi, (Ed.) *Biomechanics and Related Engineering Topics.* London: Pergamon.

PLAGENHOEF, S.C. (1966). Methods for obtaining kinetic data to analyze human motions. *Res. Quart.*, **37**, 103-112.

PLAGENHOEF, S.C. (1971). *Patterns of Human Motion.* New Jersey: Prentice Hall.

SMITH, A.J. (1972). A study of forces on the body in athletic activities with particular reference to jumping. Unpublished Ph.D. Thesis, University of Leeds, Dept. of Physical Education.

WATERLAND, J.C. (1968). Integration of Movements. *Zürich, Vol 2.,* 178-187.

WILLIAMS, M. & LISSNER, H.R. (1966). *Biomechanics of Human Motion.* Philadelphia: Saunders.

**Appendix.**

**Suppliers of cine equipment**

**(i) Cameras**

Rank Film Equipment, Audio-Visual Ltd,
P.O. Box 70, Great West Rd., Brentford, Middx.
(Arriflex Camera)

Telford Products Ltd,
4 Wadsworth Rd., Greenford, Middx.
(Milliken Camera)

Johnsons of Hendon,
Hendon Way, London, N.W.4
(Bolex Camera)

Vinten-Mitchell
Bury St. Edmunds, Suffolk.
(Mitchell Camera)

Beaulieu Cinema Ltd.,
234 Baker St., London N.W.1

## (ii) Analysing projectors

John Hadland Ltd.,
Newhouse Laboratories, Bovingden, Herts
(Specto and Vanguard projectors)


## (iii) X-Y Analysers

D-Mac Ltd.,
Queen Elizabeth Ave., Glasgow, S.W.2

P.C.D. Ltd.,
219 Sycamore Rd., Farnborough, Hants.

University Computing Co. Ltd.,
School Lane, Chandlers Ford, Hants.


## (iv) Cine Film

e.g. Kodak Ltd., P.O. Box 14, Hemel Hempstead, Herts.


## (v) Film processing

e.g. G. Humphries & Co. Ltd.,
13 Croydon House,
Croydon St., Leeds 11, Yorks.


## (vi) Stroboscopes and digital timers

Dawe Instruments Ltd.,
Concord Rd., Western Ave., London, W.3.

# 2
# RECORDING OF MOVEMENT WITHOUT PHOTOGRAPHY

Section

# RECORDING OF MOVEMENT WITHOUT PHOTOGRAPHY

by D.L. MITCHELSON

## Introduction

Photographic techniques for recording movement have enjoyed extensive use in many fields of research. Historically photography was one of the earliest means of obtaining a comprehensive and fairly accurate record of a sequence of human movement. The chief advantage of photography over many other techniques is that a complete pictorial record of the moving subject and his immediate environment is possible without requiring the use of transducing devices which may hinder movement.

Unfortunately photographic techniques suffer inherently from a number of serious shortcomings. The limitations which are placed on any particular study will depend on the type of data being sought. But one severe limitation is that of analysis time. Even when modern photogrammetric aids are used, it is a tedious process to transcribe co-ordinate data from film to a numerical form which is appropriate for further manual or computer analysis. A corollary of this is that it is never possible to monitor the film record during the movement, or to provide instantaneous feedback of the movement record via some form of display, either to the subject or to the experimenter.

Other limitations of the photographic technique are those imposed by optical parallax, line of sight constraints, and in the case of cine photography, the time resolution determined by the frame rate. These problems are discussed in detail in section 1

It is partly as a result of such difficulties that other ways of recording movement have been sought. A number of different physical principles have been used, but all of the non-photographic techniques have one feature in common; they can produce useful recordings of the movement in real time, that is to say, as the movement occurs. For many applications this single advantage is the deciding factor in choice of method.

There are, of course, other factors to be considered in making a choice between recording techniques. Most of these centre around the more technical and mathematical aspects of data aquisition and signal processing systems. It will be helpful, therefore, to spend some time in examining the general theoretical background to problems of movement recording.

## I. Theoretical Considerations

### Choice of parameters

In designing a study of human movement it is essential to be quite clear about which parameters of the movement are to be analysed and for what purpose. If one starts with careful definition of the set of parameters to be analysed, it is then possible to decide which set of parameters should be measured and which recorded directly. It does not always follow that the two sets are identical. For example, if the parameter of interest is the angular velocity of a limb segment it may well be necessary to record the movement either as an angular displacement or as an angular acceleration, and transform the primary record to angular velocity by taking the first derivative or performing an integration. The reason for this roundabout approach is simply that there is no convenient way available at present to record angular velocity of limb or body segments directly. Which of the two alternatives is chosen will depend on other considerations such as the measurement accuracy required, magnitude and orientation of the angular velocity and its relationship to other parameters of the movement that may be under examination.

Implicit in the choice of parameters which are to be recorded is the specification of acceptable levels of accuracy and frequency response. Only after the measurement requirements have been specified in this way should a particular measurement technique be chosen. Often a certain method of recording is chosen because it happens to be readily available to the researcher; little attention having been paid to the characteristics of the data that will result. The researcher then finds himself in the position of having a large quantity of recorded data which is in a form ill-suited to his intended analysis. It is then necessary to carry out tedious manual transformations or to develop a computer program to do so. It is likely that these transformations will lead to a reduction in the accuracy of the data. Unfortunately, the time and cost involved in carrying out such remedies may well be greater than that required to install the more appropriate equipment in the first place.

The sequence of decisions which must be made and the general categories of choice are conveniently summarized in Table 1. On the whole the table is self-explanatory, and may be regarded as a check-list to aid in experimental design and the selection of instrumentation. Some of the factors to be taken into account when deciding between the alternative options which are listed will now be examined.

Table 1 Factors relevant to the design of a system for movement analysis

| | | | |
|---|---|---|---|
| Movement Parameters | Co-ordinate system | Cartesian | 1, 2 or 3 dimensions |
| | | Polar | 1 or 2 planes |
| | Derivative | Position | x , x |
| | | Velocity | $\frac{dx}{dt}$ , $\dot{x}$ |
| | | Acceleration | $\frac{d^2 x}{dt^2}$ , $\ddot{x}$ |
| | | Jerk | $\frac{d^3 x}{dt^3}$ , $\dddot{x}$ |
| Signal Parameters | Mode | Continuous | Analogue |
| | | Sampled | Analogue or digital |
| | Resolution | Position resolution | Constant errors |
| | | | Linearity |
| | | | Signal to noise ratio |
| | | Time resolution | Frequency response |
| | | | Sampling rate |
| | | | Synchronisation |

## Movement Parameters

It is first necessary to establish whether the primary purpose of the study is to analyse aspects of the relative movement between various parts of the body or to look at particular movements referred to a fixed reference system. Of course, it is often necessary to do both. In which case, the relative movement between different limb or body segments can be derived by addition or subtraction of the absolute co-ordinates of the separate segments. It must be noted, however, that if this approach is adopted the accuracy of the relative measurement will suffer in either or both of two ways. Firstly the error of measurement in the absolute co-ordinates will accumulate to produce a greater error in the relative measurement. Secondly, if the movement co-ordinates are being sampled at successive instants in time, rather than being monitored continuously then the various errors which can result from using signal sampling techniques (i.e. frequency aliasing, time skewing, etc.) may be magnified considerably. The problems of signal sampling will be discussed later, but it is worth noting that the choice between alternative options in Table 1 cannot be made entirely independently. Of the techniques now available only electrogoniometry is capable of recording the relative movements of limb or body segments directly; and this only on adjacent segments.

### Co-ordinate System

The co-ordinate system which is adopted for description of the movement will, to a large extent, determine which technique cannot be used. For example, if the recordings are made in Cartesian co-ordinates and the motion of at least two reference points on each limb segment are monitored, then it is possible to obtain a record of the angular movement of the segment by carrying out a simple trigonometrical transformation. On the other hand recording the angular movement of limb segments alone would not allow the derivation of Cartesian co-ordinate data. So Cartesian co-ordinate recording systems must always be used if Cartesian data is required, but when recordings of only angular movement is wanted then either angular or Cartesian co-ordinate recordings can be used. In the Cartesian system one has a straightforward choice of using one, two or three dimensions depending on what type of movement is being studied. Recordings in three dimensions are capable, in principle, of completely specifying the movement. That is, sufficient information is preserved that using appropriate transformation, any movement characteristics may be derived.

### Time Derivatives

For some applications it is not necessary to know how a sequence of movements is related to time. For example, the measurement of maximum reach envelopes or the relationship between the movement of different limb segments need not involve a knowledge of the course of the movements with time. But there are many applications in which it is important to express the movement parameters as functions of time.

In perceptual motor skills there is a relationship between speed and accuracy of movement. The nature of the relationship is of considerable interest to those studying industrial work skills, sports skills and to the experimental psychologists studying the way in which perception and motor output are mediated by the central nervous system. In addition, it is important in bio-mechanical studies to be able to calculate the linear and angular velocities and accelerations experienced by body segments and joints so that the stress placed on the bones, joints, muscles and ligaments during high levels of physical effort can be assessed. Of course, this is especially important for studies of maximal effort in sport or heavy industrial work.

There are two basic ways in which movement can be expressed as a function of time. The first and simplest, is to define the value of a particular co-ordinate at successive points in time. This may be as a result of a sampling procedure of discreet increments in time, t, or it may be a continuous functional relationship, depending on the measurement technique employed. The relationship between the co-ordinate, x, and time, t, may look like that shown in curve 1 of Fig. 1.

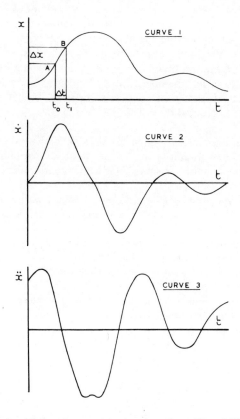

Fig. 1. Curves showing (1) function x, plotted against time, (2) and (3), corresponding 1st and 2nd time derivative of x.

The other way in which movement can be expressed is as a rate of change with respect to time. Clearly as the point defined by x moves it undergoes changes in position. If during the time interval $\Delta t$ between times $t_0$ and $t_1$, the point moves a distance $\Delta x$ then the mean rate of change in position during this interval is $\Delta x / \Delta t$. This is the *mean* velocity of the point between times $t_0$ and $t_1$. On the graph it is represented by the gradient of the line AB. If the interval $\Delta t$ is made smaller until it approaches zero then the ratio $\Delta x / \Delta t$ approaches the instantaneous value of the velocity of the point at time $t_0$, and is represented on the graph by the gradient of the tangent to the curve at time $t_0$. The convenient notation for the instantaneous rate of change of a variable x with respect to time is $\dot{x}$. Looking at the graph it is obvious that the velocity, $\dot{x}$, changes as time increases. So that $\dot{x}$ is itself a function of time and can be plotted in a similar fashion as $\dot{x}$. Curve 2 shows a plot of $\dot{x}$ against time for the same movement that is depicted in curve 1. Careful comparison will show that at a given instant of time the value of $\dot{x}$ in curve 2 corresponds to the gradient of the curve 1.

It is important to realize that the movement which is described by curves 1 and 2 is one and the same movement simply described in different ways. (However, some of the information present in the original data is lost when going from lower to higher time derivatives.) Similarly, it is possible to derive a graph of the rate of change of the velocity with respect to time, or the acceleration, which is denoted by $\ddot{x}$. This is shown in curve 3.

It is possible in principle to obtain the time derivative of any degree in this way. Usually, the acceleration is the highest derivative of interest, though the third derivative $\dddot{x}$ is sometimes wanted. This is the rate of change of acceleration, sometimes called 'jerk'.

Although, as stated above, a time derivative of any particular degree can be transformed into the derivative of higher degree some of the errors which exist in the original data are likely to be magnified in the process of transformation. So in general it is advisable to measure the parameter of interest directly. As well as minimizing the possibility of error in the final data this will also avoid the additional cost of the equipment or computing power needed to carry out the transformations.

Suppose that the actual movement that is being measured is represented by some function of time f(t) which gives the position, x, of a point at any time t. So that, quite simply,

$$x = f(t)$$

However, there are invariably some errors which arise out of the imperfections of the measuring instruments. These errors may be separated into three main types: those which are functions of time g(t), those which are functions of position h(x), and those which are independent of either (i.e. constant errors) c.

The value of x that is measured is thus defined by

$$x = f(t) + g(t) + h(x) + c$$

(1)

This equation holds good if x starts at a value of zero. But if the starting point for the movement is some fixed position, say k, then the full expression for x is

$$x = f(t) + g(t) + h(x) + c + k$$

Of course, there may be some errors which are functions f(x, t) of position and time. These will not be included in the analysis because they will render it unnecessarily complex and because the precautions taken to minimize the effect of g(t) and h(x) will usually tend to minimize the effects of any error function f(x, t) also.

Now if we differentiate both sides of equation (1) w.r.t. time, to obtain velocity, we have:

$$\dot{x} = \frac{df(t)}{dt} + \frac{dg(t)}{dt}$$

(2)

It will be seen that the errors h(x) and c have been eliminated but the information about the value of the constant k has also been lost. The only error term in equation (2) is $\frac{dg(t)}{dt}$.

At first sight it might seem that the overall error has been reduced by this transformation from position to velocity. Appearances are deceptive. It all depends on the frequency spectrum of g(t) compared to that of f(t). The amplitude of g(t) might be very small for all values of t but if g(t) is a rapidly varying function of time (as will be the case if high frequency components are present) then $\frac{dg(t)}{dt}$ can reach very high values indeed compared to $\frac{df(t)}{dt}$.

This situation is well illustrated by Fig. 2.

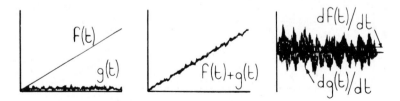

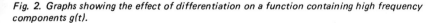

*Fig. 2. Graphs showing the effect of differentiation on a function containing high frequency components g(t).*

It will be remembered that the value of x is proportional to the gradient of the x − t curve, So while the amplitude of g(t) is shown to be very small compared to the amplitude of f(t), the gradient of the rapidly varying g(t) vs t graph is often much greater than that of f(t) vs t graph.

The magnitude of this source of error can be reduced by an appropriate choice of filter to suppress the high frequency components in g(t). Ideally if the movements under investigation have frequency components up to some value of fc and if all frequencies above this are eliminated from g(t) by filtering then the relative magnitude of the errors in $\dot{x}$ will be about the same as in x. That is to say the ratio

$$\left\{\frac{dg(t)}{dt}\right\} \Bigg/ \left\{\frac{df(t)}{dt}\right\} \quad \text{will be about the same as the ratio}$$
$$g(t) \Bigg/ f(t)$$

The ratios will not be exactly equal except in the unusual circumstances of f(t) being wholly comprised of one frequency fc and the frequency components above and below this being filtered out of g(t). Of course, in reality it is not possible to eliminate all frequency components above or below some cut off frequency while maintaining full and faithful reproduction within the cut off. In practice the effect of filtering is more accurately defined in Figure 3. The problems of signal processing, including filtering, will be dealt with later in this chapter, but it is well to remember that although the error component in a velocity record can be reduced to some extent, it can seldom be reduced to the relative level of error in the original position data. This emphasises what was said earlier about the advisability of measuring the parameter of interest directly.

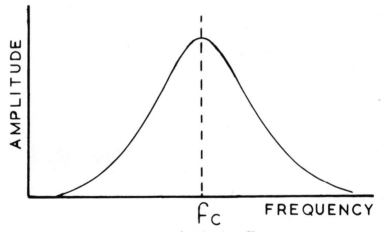

Fig. 3. Typical frequency response curve for a bandpass filter.

If, rather than transforming position data to velocity data, we had started with velocity data as the directly measured variable and wished to obtain position data from it, then another type of problem would arise. Returning to equation 2 we must assume additional measurement error terms u(x) and v, where u(x) is some function of velocity and v is a constant measurement error.

$$x = f(t) + g(t) + \int u(\dot{x})dt + \int v\,dt + w \qquad (3)$$

where w is a constant of integration.

Just as in differentiating, it was the high frequency noise, or error, which caused most trouble, when integrating it is the low frequency and constant errors which accumulate to form the greatest source of error. The terms g(t) and u(ẋ)dt will normally be of minor importance in equation 3. This is because g(t) usually arises from noise in the electronics of the instrumentation and it is typically at higher frequencies than those of interest in movement analysis. With most equipment now available any velocity dependent errors which comprise the term u(x)dt will be very small. This kind of error is only of significance in sampled data systems if high levels of velocity are reached. But the term ∫vdt may become quite large. If the integration is carried out the term becomes vt and it is apparent that the size of the error is proportional to the length of time that the movement is measured. This phenomenon is called drift and it is present in all analog electronic data processing systems which operate down to DC (i.e. are capable of handling data values which change very slowly with time). Nowadays good quality DC and chopper amplifiers are available which have negligable drift over periods of many minutes. However, it is always important to check the extent of DC drift to be expected from any particular system over the time period to be used for measurement.

Perhaps the greatest problem in using integration to obtain position data from velocity data is the unknown value of the constant of integration, w. Unless there is some means of determining the position x directly at one particular instant then equation 3 can only be used to define relative positions at different times. In practice it is sometimes possible to specify the starting position of a movement so that at time t = 0, x - w = known starting position. However, it is not always easy to arrange things in this way, particularly if several points on the body are being monitored in 2 or 3 dimensions.

So far we have only dealt with one-step transformation from position to velocity and vice versa. It is quite possible to perform double differentiation or double integration so that acceleration can be derived from position data or position from acceleration. The processes involved are exactly the same as for one-step transformations except that they are repeated one more time. Of course, the errors which occur are similarly cascaded and can assume quite enormous magnitudes. Since the error components tend in practise to occupy higher frequency bands than the movements being studied it is the author's experience that double integrations from acceleration data to position data may be usefully performed given sufficient care; but it is often futile to attempt to derive acceleration data from position data with any satisfactory degree of accuracy.

## Signal Processing

Since all the movement measuring techniques to be described in this chapter produce electrical ouput signals which represent movement parameters in some way, it will be helpful to examine some of the general principles of signal processing which many of the measuring instruments employ.

It is not within the scope of this book to give a detailed account of the various signal processing techniques, these will be found in some of the excellent texts listed at the end of the chapter. For those who intend to undertake experimental work in human movement it is essential to understand the theory and application of certain aspects of signal processing very thoroughly. The intention of this section is to list which areas are important and give a brief indication of why.

A movement parameter can be represented by an electrical signal in a number of ways. But there are two broad categories of choice. These are the choice between analogue and digital and the choice between continuous or sampled measurements. In general an analogue signal may be continuous or sampled whereas a digital signal results necessarily from a data sampling procedure and changes value in discreet little jumps.

Signals which are voltage analogues of a movement parameter are the easiest to understand and to process. By employing relatively simple analogue electronic circuits based on operational amplifiers it is possible to add or subtract two or more signals. This is useful for obtaining a record of the relative movement of different parts of the body.

Analogue multipliers and dividers are also available and these make it possible to compute the ratios of one movement parameter to another. Analogue circuits generally have the advantage of being relatively simple and virtually instantaneous in the operations which they perform. This means that they can be made to reproduce analogues of movement up to quite high frequencies. Reproduction of movements with frequency components up to at least 10 KHz is easily obtained to an accuracy of .1% of the range of movement under study. Higher bandwidths than this are quite possible but seldom required for movement analysis. In fact it is often the case that higher frequencies are of little interest and need to be filtered out. To do this, analogue filter circuits exist which will attenuate signals of higher than a predetermined frequency. The ideal frequency response of one kind of filter, called a low pass filter, would look like the solid line in Fig. 4.

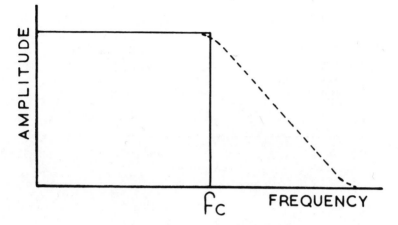

*Fig.4. Typical frequency response curve for a low pass filter.*

All the frequency components below the critical frequency fc would be passed on without attenuation, but all frequencies higher than fc would be completely suppressed. In practise this ideal performance cannot be obtained and the actual frequency response of the filter will look like the dotted line. The sloping part of the curve is called the roll-off characteristic of the filter, and is usually defined in terms of db per octave.

The attenuation of high frequency components in a signal is often a necessity when sampled data systems are used. Any signal components present which have a higher frequency than $\pi fs$, where fs is the sampling rate, can produce an apparent signal at lower than the frequency $\pi fs$. This effect is known as 'aliasing', that is, the high frequency signals presented to the input of the sampling device masquerade as lower frequency signals at the output.

Aliasing can be an insiduous source of error in movement analysis using sampled data systems. The problem is that unless the complete frequency spectrum of the incoming signals is known, an experimenter may be blissfully unaware that aliasing is taking place. What appear to be good recordings may contain quite unacceptable errors.

The way in which aliasing occurs can best be explained with reference to Fig. 5.

One common form of aliasing which most people have observed is the 'wagon wheel' effect in films. Since the frame rate of the film is usually much lower than the frequency at which the spokes of a wheel pass any one point, aliasing takes place and the wheels appear to turn either much more slowly than they really are, or even seem to go backwards sometimes.

The best way to safeguard against the possibility of aliasing in recording movement via electronic signals is to insert a cut-off filter at a point in the

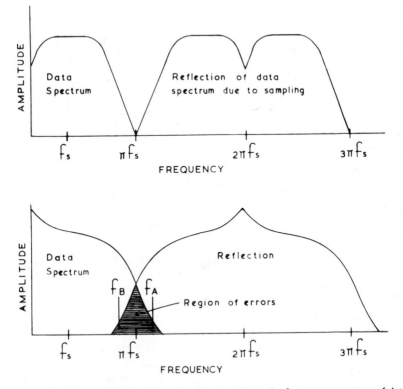

*Fig. 5. Aliasing in sampled data. The upper diagram shows the frequency spectrum of data signals which just fall within $\pi f_s$. The data spectrum in the lower diagram overlaps $\pi f_s$, thus producing a region of confusion with the reflected spectrum, a frequency $f_A$ in the data spectrum which is greater than $\pi f_s$ aliases as a frequency $f_B$ below $\pi f_s$.*

circuit before the sampling occurs. The roll-off characteristics of the filter should be chosen so that the amplitude of signals at frequencies above the sampling rate are negligably small, i.e. less than the resolution amplitude required, while at the same time imposing no attenuation on signals at the frequencies of the movement under study.

In some techniques described later in this chapter the sampling operation takes place right at the input of the measuring device, e.g. in CODA. In cases like this it is not possible to filter the signal prior to sampling. The remedy is to design the equipment to have a sampling frequency well above any frequency components which may reasonably be expected in the input signal. This means that the sampling rate is not determined by the highest frequency components in the movement but by factors which may introduce even higher frequency components such as a loosely mounted transducing device being set into an unwanted oscillatory mode, or AC mains interference, etc.

In the author's opinion, 150Hz would be a minimum acceptable sampling rate for most human movement analysis purpose, and a rate of 1 KHz would be preferred.

## II Some Modern Techniques for Recording Movement without Photography

It is not the intention of this chapter to deal with all of the non-photographic techniques for recording movement which are available, but rather to present details of some of the newer techniques which promise to provide more powerful means of analysis than has been possible with earlier methods. Useful texts on other non-photographic techniques such as electrogoniometry are listed in the references at the end of this chapter.

### Polarised Light Goniometer

This general technique was announced almost simultaneously by Grieve (1969) and Reed & Reynolds (1969). Grieve named his device Polgon. It was not necessarily intended that this name should refer to other types of instrument which employ polarised light to measure angular parameters of limb movement, but it is such a convenient contraction of the title of this section that it will probably be used to describe all such instruments.

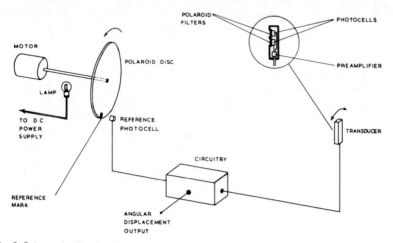

*Fig. 6. Schematic diagram of the Polarised Light Goniometer.*

A laboratory prototype polgon was developed at the Department of Ergonomics and Cybernetics* at Loughborough University of Technology in 1970. It is this device which provides the basis for the description of the technique which follows.

The light emitted from a DC light source is polarised by transmission through a disc of linearly polarising filter. The disc is mounted on the drive shaft of a small electric motor and made to rotate at a rate of 150 revolutions per second. The beam of light which is thus transmitted is plane polarised, with its plane of polarisation being rotated through one complete revolution every .0067 seconds. The light is received by a transducer which consists of a photo-cell in front of which is mounted a small disc of polarising filter of the same type as used in the large rotating disc. As the plane of polarisation of the light beam rotates, alternate extinction and transmission takes place at the filters in the transducer, thus producing a sinusoidal light flux into the detecting photo-cell. Since the extinction and transmission occur twice for each revolution of the disc, the frequency of the signal received at the photo-cell is twice the rate of revolution of the disc.

A small rectangular opaque reference mark is mounted on the edge of the rotating disc, and another photo-cell is fixed near the edge of the disc in line of sight to the filament of the light source. Consequently, every time the reference mark on the disc passes in front of the photo-cell, obscuring the light, a pulse is generated in the photo-cell.

Both the reference pulse and the sinusoidal signal from the transducer are passed to an electronic circuit which measures the elapsed time between the reference pulse and the following zero crossing of the sinusoidal signal. This time measurement is then converted to a DC voltage which is proportional to the angular displacement between the polarising axis of the filter in the transducer, and the angular position of the photo-cell which senses the reference mark on the disc.

The essential elements of the circuitry are illustrated in block diagram form in Figure 7. The signal from the transducer is first fed to an amplifier which has a twin-T filter network in its feedback loop. This allows the amplifier to be tuned to the frequency of the incoming sinusoidal signal, thus reducing the unwanted frequency components of the signal which may arise from room lighting and mains pickup. The amplified and filtered signal is then fed to a comparator. The output from the comparator is a square wave which switches from a logic level of 0 to a logic level of 1 each time the sine wave input crosses the zero reference voltage level in a negative going sense. The comparator output switches from logical 1 to logical 0 when the sine wave crosses zero in the positive direction.

Meanwhile the signal from the photo-cell which senses the reference mark on the polarising disc is first fed to an amplifier and then to a monostable logic

*Now, Department of Human Sciences.

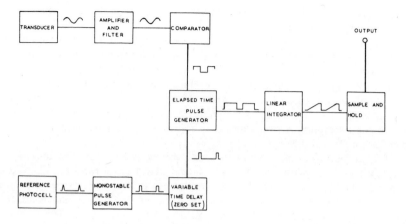

*Fig. 7. Block diagram of Polarised Light Goniometer circuit.*

circuit which produces a short duration pulse which is compatible with other logic input requirement of the circuit. This signal is then fed to another monostable element whose time constant may be adjusted by means of a variable resistor. The effect of this is to introduce a time delay between the generation of the reference pulse and its transmission to later stages of the circuitry. The ability to adjust this time delay effectively provides a zero setting function by which the output signal of the circuit may be offset to any desired initial angular value.

Both the reference pulse and the output from the comparator are fed to the input of a bistable logic circuit which is set to logical 1 by the reference pulse and to logical 0 by the next negative going edge of the square wave from the comparator. The resulting output from the bistable element is a square wave signal which remains in the logical 1 state for a period of time which is proportional to the angular displacement of the transducer from the angular position of the reference photo-cell. This elapsed time signal is then used to control the length of time for which a linear integrator is allowed to ramp up from zero volts.

The slope of the ramp is determined by a fixed input reference voltage, $E_i$, and by the value of the input resistor R and feed-back capacitor C. The value of the integrator ouput $E_o$ is given by

$$E_o = \frac{1}{-RC} \int E_i \, dt$$

Hence

$$\frac{d\,E_o}{dt} = \frac{-E_i}{RC}$$

Values of Ei, R and C were chosen so that the full scale value of Eo representing $180°$ is 1.8 volts.

The amplitude which the ramp has reached at the end of the elapsed time signal is maintained for 2 milliseconds by keeping the integrator in the 'hold' condition. The integrator is then re-set to zero ready for the next ramping period. During this 2 millisecond period, the amplitude of the output level of the integrator is sampled by a sample and hold element. This DC level is then held constant at the output of the sample land hold circuit until the next 2 millisecond sampling period when it is adjusted to the peak level of the next ramp from the integrator.

The output from the circuit is a DC voltage proportional to the angular displacement of the transducer at that instant, within one revolution period of the polarising disc, at which the light arriving at the photo-cell of the transducer is at its half maximum value. It is also apparent that the output level is updated once in each revolution period of the disc. When the transducer is made to rotate in a plane parallel to the disc, then the output appears as a 'staircase' signal of step length equal to one period of revolution of the disc.

The design of the transducer required considerable care in order to ensure a minimum of unwanted noise due to mains and radio pick-up and due to extraneous light signals being received at the photo-cells. The latter effect was greatly reduced by use of a pair of photo-cells which were closely matched for sensitivity. The circuit of the transducers is shown in Figure 8. It can be seen that the photo-cells are connected so that their outputs work in opposition to each other. The extrance window of each photo-cell is covered by linearly polarising filter, with the plane of polarisation of the filters being at right angles to each other within the same plane. This design means that any non-polarised light which is incident on the two photo-cells is transmitted in equal amounts to each, and the resulting signals from the two cells thus cancel each other. On the other hand, the polarised beam of light which is incident at the photo-cell is first transmitted to one cell and extinguished at the other, and then vice-versa, as the plane of polarisation of the beam rotates. The signals from the two cells are thus complementary.

All of the components in the transducer are of miniature type so that the overall physical dimensions are kept to 5 x 1.5 x .5 cm. and the mass kept down to 15 gm. In this way the extent to which the transducers interfere with the normal movement patterns of the subject is minimised.

In order to provide both electrical shielding and mechanical strength, the transducers are contained in light weight aluminium cases, which are electrically connected to signal ground.

The transducers are connected to the main circuitry by means of lightweight, flexible cable, consisting of two conductors and a braided shield. Once again, this keeps the human subject as free from encumbrance as possible.

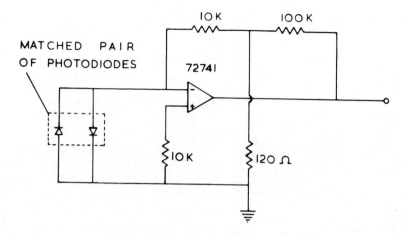

*Fig. 8. Circuit of limb mounted transducer.*

## Angular Velocity Circuitry

In order to provide on-line output of signals which are proportional to the angular velocity of the transducers, some additional circuitry was designed. Its principle of operation is based on calculating the derivative of a function by the method of finite differences. That is, the signal levels of each consecutive pair of samples of the angular displacement signal are compared. A signal which is proportional to their difference, d$\phi$ is then presented at the output of the angular velocity circuit. If dt is the sampling period, then the angular velocity, v$\phi$, is given by

$$v\phi = \frac{d\phi}{dt}$$

Thus, if d$\phi$ is in degrees, the output of the velocity circuit must be multiplied by a factor $^1$/dt in order to give v$\phi$ in degrees per second. In practice since the sampling period is determined by the projector disc revolution rate of 150 revolutions per second, then:

$$^1/dt = 150$$

Thus the output of the angular velocity circuit must be amplified by a factor of 150.

Figure 9. shows a block diagram of the angular velocity circuit. The angular displacement signal is split at the input, being fed to a sample and hold element

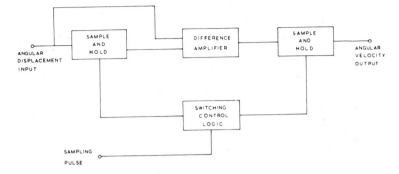

*Fig. 9. Block diagram of angular velocity circuit.*

and to a line which by-passes the sample and hold element. A triggering pulse derived from the reference photo-cell of the projector provides the clock pulse for switching logic circuitry, which in turn controls the operating mode of the sample and hold elements. The timing sequence of the mode switching is arranged so that the input signal is sampled at the end of each angular displacement sampling period. The output from the sample and hold element and the unprocessed input signal are fed to an operational amplifier. Since the input signal is inverted by the sample and hold element, the output of the amplifier is proportional to the difference between the real time input signal sampled at the end of the previous sampling period. This operational amplifier also provides the gain of 150 which is required to make the angular velocity output voltage equal to the angular displacement output voltage when the angular displacement in degrees, and the angular velocity, in degrees per second, are numerically equal.

The output from the operational amplifier is fed to another sample and hold element which holds the signal at this level for one sampling period. The switching logic circuit updates the sample and hold element in the middle of the angular displacement sampling period. In this way, the velocity output is held constant during the step discontinuity that occurs at the end of each angular displacement sampling period. The angular velocity output is thus a 'staircase' signal of the same step width as the angular displacement signal, but lagging it by one sampling period.

It is possible to operate two such angular velocity circuits in series in order to obtain an angular acceleration output. The main difficulty in doing this however, is that at each stage of differentiation there is a large increase in the noise level of the output signal. The reason for this may be understood if it is supposed that the angular displacement is held at some fixed value. Then both the angular velocity and angular acceleration outputs would be zero. But in each of the velocity circuits there is an overall gain factor of 150. Consequently any noise which is present on the angular displacement output is multiplied by 150 at each stage.

Since the measured noise level at the angular displacement output is in the region of 0.3 degrees, it follows that the noise level at the angular velocity output is equivalent to 45 degrees per second. This high level of noise would be of little importance in monitoring slow movements but would be unacceptable in measurement of the fast angular movements encountered in many athletic skills. Of course, the angular acceleration output would have the absurd noise value of 6750 degrees per second per second.

### Factors affecting accuracy (Noise, Linearity, Geometry)

The main possible sources of noise appearing at the output of the apparatus are optical noise introduced at the transducer photo-cells, electromagnetic interference from the mains and radio stations, etc., and the mechanical vibrations or irregularities in the rate of rotation of the polarising disc.

The most useful way of assessing the effect of noise on the performance of the apparatus is to calculate the expected noise level for the worst case and also for the expected normal operating condition.

The worst case noise contribution from optical effects will occur when the transducer photo-cells are mismatched in optical sensitivity by the maximum of 10% allowed in their specified performance characteristics, and when the 100 Hz component of the room fluorescent lighting exceeds the amplitude of the polarised beam signal. Since the light source in the projector is rated at 75 watts, the latter condition would occur when the transducer is about equidistant from the normal 100 watt room lighting and the projector and inclined at about equal angles to both.

Under these conditions the ratio of signal to noise at the output of the transducer would be 10:1. The twin T filter in the feedback loop of the first amplifier in the main circuitry then provides a relative attenuation of the unwanted 100 Hz frequencies of 20:1, compared to the signal at the tuned frequency of 300 Hz. The worst case signal to noise ratio at the output of the first main amplifier is thus 200:1. The way in which this alters the time when the sinusoidal signal crosses zero, and hence the equivalent angular error at the output, may be determined by simple calculation.

If S is the instantaneous level of the signal at time t, then

$$S = K(200 \sin wt + \sin \frac{wt}{3})$$

where K is some constant gain factor and w is the signal frequency (300 Hz) and w/3 is the noise frequency (100 Hz). The formula assumes that the noise component due to the room fluorescent lights is sinusoidal and of 100 Hz frequency. This has been checked by observing the signal from one photo-cell illuminated only by room lights, and was found to be the case.

The value of S at each zero crossing of the signal is zero, hence

$$200 \sin wt + \sin w/3t = 0$$

Making use of the identity,

$$\sin 3x = 3 \sin x - 4 \sin^3 x$$

we have,

$$200 (3 \sin \frac{wt}{3} - 4 \sin^3 \frac{wt}{3}) + \sin \frac{wt}{3} = 0$$

i.e.

$$601 \sin \frac{wt}{3} = 800 \sin^3 \frac{wt}{3}$$

i.e.

$$\sin \frac{wt}{3} = 0. \text{ or } \sin \frac{wt}{3} = (\frac{601}{800})^{\frac{1}{2}}$$

Hence

$$wt = 0 \text{ or } \pm 180^\circ \ 15'$$

In the absence of noise the signal would cross the zero voltage level of increments of $\pi$ radians, or 180 degrees. So for the above case the maximum error is $\pm 15'$ of arc, or 0.25 degrees.

In practice the level of optical interference is much lower than this since the light from the polarising projector which is incident at the transducers is normally at least ten times greater in magnitude than the light from the room lights.

The noise contribution due to electromagnetic interference cannot be predicted by calculation and neither can the mechanical noise in the rotation of the disc. However, the combined effect of these two noise sources was judged by placing the transducers very near to the projector and well shielded from other light sources. This reduced optical interference to zero. By feeding the output to an oscilloscope whose time base was triggered by the mains frequency, it was possible to observe the amplitude of the 50 Hz mains frequency interference and also the remaining higher frequency mechanical noise components super imposed. The amplitude of the mains interference was equivalent to 0.08 degrees of arc, and that of the mechanical noise, less than 0.05 degrees of arc.

The maximum r.m.s. noise that may be expected is thus given by the square root of the sum of the squares of each noise component, i.e. r.m.s. noise - 0.27 degrees of arc.

The linearity of the output signal as a function of the angular position of the transducer is dependent on the uniform quality of polarising filter over its total area; on the constancy of the angular velocity of the disc, and on the linearity of the ramping integrator in the main circuitry. It was found relatively easy to design the instrument so that the total deviation from linearity due to these factors combined was no more than $\pm .1\%$ over the $180^\circ$ range.

## Geometric Factors Affecting Accuracy

For ease of reference in discussing geometrical factors which determine accuracy, the plane in which the polarising filters of the transducer are fixed will be called the primary transducer plane, and a line in that plane which joins that mid-point of each of the two filters will be called the primary transducer axis.

When the primary transducer plane is perpendicular to the line of sight from transducer to projector, then the output will be directly proportional to the angular displacement of the primary transducer axis within the primary transducer plane. If, however, the transducer is turned about any other axis than the line of sight, it is not immediately apparent how this will affect the output signal. In Figure 10 a momentarily frozen projected light beam is indicated with its plane of polarisation vertical.

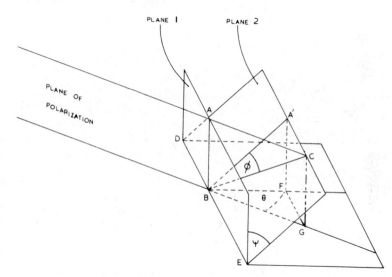

Fig. 10. Diagram illustrating the error angle $\phi$, due to the two rotations of the transducer $\psi$ and $\theta$.

If the primary transducer plane is rotated about AB, the transducer axis, by some angle $\theta$ to position indicated as plane 1 in the Figure, then the plane of polarisation still cuts the transducer through the line AB. Consequently, the linearity of the output is unaffected. Similar reasoning holds if the primary transducer plane starts in the position normal to the line of sight and is subsequently rotated about a horizontal axis normal to the plane of polarisation, Again, the linearity of the output is maintained. If, however, a combination of these two rotations takes place, then errors in the output will occur.

Returning to Figure 10, with the primary transducer plane in the position indicated by plane 1, it is already rotated about axis AB by an angle $\theta$. If, now, it is rotated about axis DE through an angle to the position indicated as plane 2, then the intersection of the plane of polarisation with the primary transducer plane no longer lies on the primary transducer axis A'B', but is displaced by an angle $\phi$ to the position of CB. The angle $\phi$ is thus the angular error at the output resulting from the two axis rotation of the transducer. This is the kind of error which will occur if, for example, the transducer were mounted on the lower arm in order to record angular movements in the sagittal plane, and the subject also made arm movements in a horizontal plane together with pronation-supination twists of the arm. From Figure 10 it is easy to calculate $\phi$.

Tan $\phi$ = A'C/A'B
But A'C = FG (vertical projection)
and Sin $\psi$ = BF/A'B and tan $\theta$ = FG/BF
    $\therefore$ Tan $\phi$ = Sin $\psi$ tan $\theta$
thus if $\psi = 20°$ and $\theta = 20°$
then $\phi = 7°$

This is an error of much greater proportions than any of the other errors in the system. It is therefore most important to ensure that the projector is placed in such a configuration in relation to the movement of the subject that angular displacements of the transducer of either the $\psi$ or $\theta$ type, or both should be restricted to an amount which keeps the error $\phi$ within the limits of accuracy required for a particular application.

The graph in Figure 11 shows a family of curves of the angular displacement error $\phi$ as a function of $\theta$ at discrete values of $\psi$. This may be used as an aid to estimate the maximum geometric errors which may occur for any proposed experimental design.

### Typical application of Polgon technique

While this technique may be applied in a variety of different ways, two examples have been chosen which serve to illustrate its unique advantage, i.e. the facility of recording angular movement relative to a fixed reference, either as a function of time, or as a function of the angular attitude of other limbs.

### Investigation of arm-trunk co-ordination

In the first example recordings are made as a function of time. A simulated light industrial assembly task was used to study the relationship between arm,

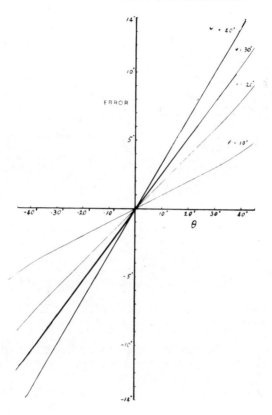

*Fig. 11. Measured values of displacement error φ, plotted as a function of θ at discrete values of ψ.*

trunk and head movements when reaching for objects placed at various positions on a work surface. The experimental arrangement is illustrated in Figure 12.

The subject was seated at the table with his sagittal plane normal to the line-of-sight to the projector. Transducers were mounted on the upper arm, cervical spine and the head. The subject was instructed to pick up some 1 cm. diameter rubber grommets which were placed between 20 cms. and 95 cms. from the edge of the table in increments of 15 cms. The instructions emphasised that the movement should be made as the subject naturally would move when performing an assembly task, for example. Each grommet was picked up in turn and placed at the edge of the table. Then in order to simulate a simple assembly task, the grommet was threaded over a short vertical rod placed on the edge of the table to the left of the subject.

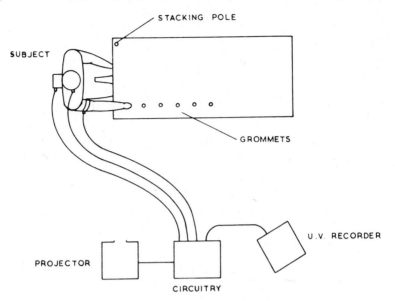

*Fig. 12. Experimental arrangement using the polarised light goniometer to study a simulated industrial assembly task.*

A total of eight subjects were used. Each subject performed two experimental runs picking up the grommets from the nearest to the farthest, in turn, and two runs starting with the farthest grommets first.

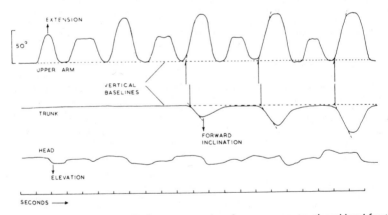

*Fig. 13. Recordings of angular displacement vs. time for upper arm, trunk and head for the simulated assembly task*

**Results**

Figure 13 shows a sample of the UV recordings of the angular attitudes of the head, cervical spine, and upper arm. The progressively greater increase in forward inclination of the spine for the more distantly placed grommets is easily seen. The most interesting result of this study however is the way in which the inclination of each spinal movement lags behind the initiation of the upper arm movement. For short reach distances there is little or no inclination of the spine. In fact, for most subjects trunk inclination does not occur until the reach distance exceeds the length of the fully extended arm. But, as shown in Figure 14 the time lag between the start of the arm and trunk movement is greatest for the smaller trunk movements, and approaches zero for the larger trunk movements.

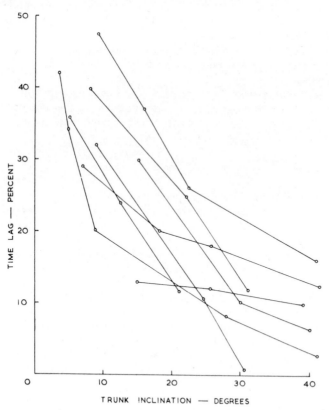

*Fig. 14. Percentage of total movement time by which the initiation of trunk movement lags the initiation of arm movement plotted vs. trunk inclination for eight subjects.*

The attitude of the head does not show quite such consistent trends, although for most subjects the angle of the head was elevated during the forward picking-up movements. Also the initiation of this head movement tended to lead the arm movement by 0.8 seconds on average.

The shape of the time lag vs trunk inclination curve tends to suggest that perceptual discrimination of the distance to be reached is an important factor in determining the phasic relationship of these kinds of arm and trunk movements. The fact that the time lag is greatest when only small inclinations of the trunk are necessary in order to reach the object implies that the subject does not perceive the need to lean forward until he has almost reached the limit of his arm extention. When required to reach far beyond his arm's length however it becomes immediately apparent that he must lean in addition to reaching, consequently he commences leaning at the same time he starts to reach.

There is room for a great deal of further study in this area. What for example is the effect of learning on these phasic time lags? Do similar effects occur in other limb movements? Can the deliberate adoption of different perceptual criteria for phasing limbs and body movements affect levels of motor skill? The Polgon technique will be a useful research tool in helping to answer some of these questions.

In the realm of athletics, it may be fruitful to use this technique to provide immediate feedback to subjects, via a suitable display, so that they can monitor particular parameters of their movements and so improve motor skills.

### Gait Analysis with Polgon.

Another application of the polgon technique which appears to be particularly valuable is in gait analysis. If the transducers are mounted on the upper and lower legs, and the respective outputs made to drive the x and y channels of an x - y plotter, then it is possible to obtain records of the gait characteristics in the form of angle to angle plots as shown in Figure 15. These particular graphs were obtained by requiring the subject to walk at a number of different speeds on a treadmill.

It will be noted that the angles which are recorded are the absolute orientations of each segment rather than the relative angle between them. This provides more complete information than is available with electrogoniometers which measure the relative angle only. It is always possible to derive the angle between segments given the separate angles of each segment relative to a fixed reference axis but it is not possible to derive the separate segment angles given only the relative angle between them.

It is not within the scope of this chapter to dwell on the precise interpretation of records such as these. However, it is worth drawing the readers

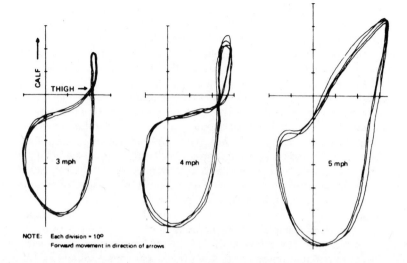

*Fig. 15. Graphs of lower leg angle vs. upper leg angle using the output from the polarised light goniometer connected on-line to an X-Y plotter. The subject performed a number of walking cycles on a treadmill at speeds of 3, 4 and 5 mph respectively.*

attention to several points. Firstly the consistency with which the movements occur at each speed is quite remarkable. For most normal subjects walking at near their accustomed pace, the movement records for several walking cycles repeat themselves within ± 2 degrees at each point in the cycle. But it can be seen that the shape of the record changes quite significantly for different walking speeds.

Grieve has found that such records are very sensitive indicators of change in motor function in the legs due to such diseases as arthritis, stroke, etc. Consequently the technique shows much promise as an instrument for diagnosis and monitoring in the field of orthapaedic medicine and in prosthetic design and assessment.

## Design study for a Cartesian Opto-electronic Dynamic Anthropometer (CODA)

In 1971 the author proposed a design for an optical instrument which would simultaneously measure the cartesian co-ordinates in three-dimensions of a number of landmarks fixed to a subject under study. The electrical output from the instrument would be in the form either of analogue or digital signals proportional to the landmark XYZ co-ordinates and which track the changing XYZ values as movement occurs. Such as instrument is now being constructed at the Department of Ergonomics at Loughborough University of Technology and it is the design objective for this apparatus which will be briefly outlined here.

The design objective was to provide outputs for the XYZ co-ordinates of eight landmarks, with a position resolution of 1 part in 4,000 and a frequency response of 200 Hz. Since the instrument repetitively samples the position of each landmark, the required frequency response of 200 Hz is achieved by using a sampling rate of 1 KHz. The landmarks are miniature infra-red light sources in the form of gallium arsenide lasers. Using such devices it is posible to obtain intense pulses of infra-red light of about 1 microsecond duration repeated at a frequency of 1 KHz. The peak power of the emitted light is about 1 watt and when properly diffused to radiate uniformly in all directions is well within safety limits for the eye laid down by the British Standards Institute ref. B.S. 4803 1972. The overall physical size of these light sources including their mounting is about 5 x 5 x 5 mm. and their mass is about 1 gm.

The position of the light sources used as landmarks is detected by a specially designed electronic camera system comprised of three cameras mounted in relation to the subject as shown in Fig. 16. The two outside cameras 1 and 3 are sensitive to horizontal movement of the landmarks in the X direction. Because these two cameras are separated by a fixed distance (100 cms.) it is possible to use the outputs from them to determine the position of the landmark in the Y direction. In effect this is rather like the stereoscopic vision of the human eyes. The computation of the Y co-ordinates is accomplished electronically within the cameras in a matter of microseconds so that the high sampling rate of 1 KHz is maintained.

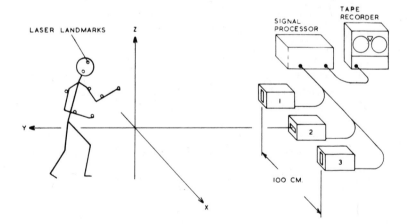

*Fig. 16. Physical arrangement of CODA cameras in relation to the subject under study.*

The third camera placed between the other two is sensitive to vertical movement only, so that after electronic computation within the instrument to compensate for the effect of distance (Y co-ordinate,) it provides the Z co-ordinate output.

The outputs so produced are proportional to the true XYZ co-ordinates of the landmarks and do not contain errors equivalent to the parallax errors which occur in normal photographic recording.

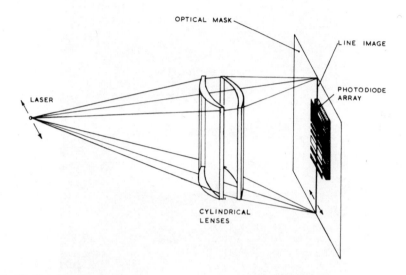

*Fig. 17. Simplified representations of the camera optics of the CODA system.*

The optical system in each of the cameras is identical and is shown in simplified form in Fig. 17. The objective lens is comprised of a cylindrical lens doublet. The landmarks, which are essentially point light sources are focused by the cylindrical lenses into a line image in the focal plane. Thus as the light source moves in the direction of the arrow transverse to the optical axis, the line moves a proportionate distance across the focal plane. An array of silicon photo-detectors is mounted in the focal plane of the camera in order to detect the position of the line image. This is facilitated by placing in front of the detector array an optical mask which has a pattern of opaque and transparent areas corresponding to the digital Gray code as shown in Fig. 18. As the line image moves across the mask only those detectors having a transparent part of the mask between them and the line receive any light. Hence the output from the first seven detectors provides a 7 bit digital signal corresponding to the position of the landmark along the transverse axis.

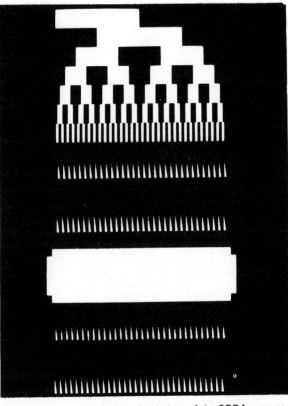

*Fig. 18. Optical mask which is used in the focal plane of the CODA cameras. The pattern at the top encodes line image coarse position in the digital Gray code; the triangular patterns in the lower part of the mask act as analogue verniers.*

Due to the finite diameter of the light sources (about 1 mm.) and the slight blurring of the image required by a large range of movement to and from the camera, the line image has a finite width which may vary between .01 and 04 mm. Since the total width of the detector array is limited by practical manufacturing reasons to about 10 mm. the digital resolution of line position is limited to .04/10, i.e. 1 part in 250. This is equivalent to eight bit digital resolution. Since 12 bit resolution is the design objective, the remaining bits of resolving accuracy are obtained by use of an analog vernier optical mask in front of four of the elements of the detector array. The vernier pattern consists of sixty-four transparent wedges for each element, with the pattern advanced by one quarter of the interval between each wedge for each of the elements, as indicated in Fig. 18. As the line image moves across any of the transparent wedges the quantity of light transmitted to the photodetector behind is linearly proportionate to the position of the line. However, since the line image may have a width of up to half the width of a wedge, this linear relationship only holds good in the centre half of each wedge. For line positions outside of this central region, the outside edges of the image will be obscured and the light received will be less than that required to maintain linearity. Due to the staggered arrangement of the rows of wedges it can be seen that the image falls in the linear region of a wedge in only one row at a time. As the line image sweeps across the focal plane, it comes into the linear region of a wedge in the first row, as it leaves this it enters the linear region of a wedge in the second row and so on through the third and fourth rows and then back to the first row, etc. The electronics is designed to detect the row in which the image is producing a linear response. This selection of one out of four rows provides an additional two bits of digital information about the position of the image. Furthermore the analog output from the detector in the row selected is digitised by means of an A to D converter and provides the last 6 bits of information about image position.

The seven bits available from the Gray code mask together with the two bits from row selection and the remaining six bits give a total of 15 bits. However, the actual resolution is only 14 bits since the least significant (i.e. seventh) bit from the Gray code mask is used to overlap the most significant bit of the 2 bit row selection in order to avoid ambiguous or erroneous matching of outputs from the digital and analogue parts of the optical system.

The 14 bit digital output from each of the camera is used to perform the digital arithmetic necessary for computing the Y co-ordinates by the stereoscopic principle mentioned earlier. Digital arithmetic is also performed to compensate for the apparent change in image size as a function of distance (i.e. Parallax compensation). Two bits of resolution are necessarily lost in this process, hence the final output resolution of the instrument is 12 bits, i.e. $2^{12}$ or 1 part in 4096.

The total angular field of view of each camera is $26°$ in horizontal and vertical axes so that the actual volume of space in which movement can be recorded will take the form of a trapezoidal solid.

The dimensions of the trapezoid and its distance from the cameras will be determined by the spacing of the outside cameras. For example, if the outside cameras are 50 cm. apart, the apex of the solid will be approximately 100 cm. away, and at a distance of 3 meters the width of the cone will be about 1.5 meters and movements of .5 mm. can be resolved.

The greatest distance at which movements can be recorded is limited by the effect of electronic noise in the photodetectors and the practical limits of light source intensity. In the system as currently envisaged, the light sources give pulses of light of 5w peak power at a wavelength of 900 nanometers, the detectors have a noise equivalent power (N.E.P.) of $10^{-10}$ watts. The optics of the cameras is such that each photodetector has an effective area of 3 mm.$^2$ Calculation shows that under these conditions the instrument can sustain the desired 12 bit resolution up to a distance of about 4 meters. This gives an effective volume for useful measurement of approximately 2 x 2 meters.

At distances greater than 3 meters the instrument loses 2 bits resolution for each doubling of the distance, i.e. it follows the inverse square law. This means that at a distance of 6 meters the resolution would be 10 bits, i.e. 1 in 1024.

While the 12 bit small signal resolution of CODA is determined by signal to noise considerations, the overall linearity of the output across the total field of view is limited by the attainable quality of the camera optics, particularly of the cylindrical lens system. Accommodating the designed 26$^\circ$ field of view on the 10 mm. wide photodetector array dictates a focal length of only 20 mm. for the lens. Under these conditions, and using a 4 mm. wide slit aperture at the lens, the best linearity that can be obtained for reasonable cost is of the order of .1%.

It is envisaged that the eight light source landmarks will be powered from a lightweight battery pack mounted on a belt around the subjects waist. Small gauge cables would then carry the current to each of the landmarks. Synchronization of the light pulses with an eight channel multiplexer in the main electronic unit in the camera console will be accomplished via short range radio, the transmitter being mounted on the console and the receiver in the subject's belt pack. This arrangement will leave the subject quite free of any electrical cables attaching him to static equipment. Thus complete 360$^\circ$ turns and similar movements can be performed without the subject getting entagled in a mesh of cables.

## Application of CODA

Since the instrument has not been constructed at the time of writing it is not possible to report the results of any experimental work based on its use. However, if it meets the designed objectives it will be possible to record and analyse the three dimensional records of movements of many types, from the finter motor skills employed in writing. for example to athletic movements carried out in large volumes of space. The main limitation of the technique will be the requirement for a clear line of sight between landmark and cameras. This will not be so difficult to achieve as with conventional three dimensional photographic recording since all three of the CODA cameras will be placed at the same side of the subject.

## References

CARLSÖÖ, S. (1972). *How Man Moves.* London: Heinemann.

FINLAY, F.R. & KARPOVICH, P.V. (1964). Electrogoniometric analysis of normal and pathological gaits. *Res. Quart.,* **35**, 379-384.

FURNEE, E.H. (1967). Hybrid instrumentation for prosthesis research. *Digest 7th Int. Conf. Med. Biol. Eng.,* Stockholm.

GOLLNICH, P. D. & KARPOVICH, P.V. (1964). Electrogoniometric studies of locomotion and of some athletic movements. *Res. Quart.,* **35**, 357-369.

KARPOVICH, P.V. & WILKLOW, L.B. (1959). A goniometric study of the human foot in standing and walking. *U.S. Armed Forces Medical J.,* **10**, 885-903.

KATTAN, A. & NADLER, G. (1969). Equations of hand motion path for work space design. *Human Factors,* **11**, 123-130.

MACY, J. (1965). Analog-Digital Conversion Systems. In Stacey & Waxman (Eds.). *Computers in Biomedical Research,* Vol.II. New York: Academic Press.

MITCHELSON, D.L. (1973). An opto-electronic technique for analysis of angular movements. In Cerquiglini, Venerando & Wartenweiler (Eds.). *Medicine and Sport, Vol. 8: Biomechanics III.* Basel: Karger.

NADLER, G. & GOLDMAN, J. (1958). The Unopar. *J. Indust. Eng.,* **9**, 58-65.

PLAGENHOEF, S.C. (1966). Methods of obtaining kinetic data to analyse human motions. *Res. Quart.,* **37**, 105-112.

TIPTON, C.M. & KARPOVICH, P.V. (1965). Electrogoniometric records of knee and ankle movements in pathological gaits. *Arch. Phys. Med. & Rehab.,* **46**, 267-272.

TOPPING, J. (1962). *Errors of Observation and Their Treatment.* London: Chapmann & Hall.


## Bibliography

GRIEVE, D.W. (1969). A device called the Polgon for the measurement of the orientation of parts of the body relative to a fixed external axis. *J. Physiol.,* **201**, 70.

REED, D.J. & REYNOLDS, P.J. (1969). A joint angle detector. *J. Applied Physiol.,* **27**, 745-748.

# 3

# COMPUTER SIMULATION OF HUMAN MOTION

# COMPUTER SIMULATION OF HUMAN MOTION*

by DORIS I. MILLER.

In this section, the computer simulation technique for studying the mechanics of human motion is discussed with particular emphasis being placed upon simulation in sport. An examination of existing models illustrates the type of research presently being undertaken. To provide further insight into the method, a detailed consideration is given to each of the steps necessary to implement a computer simulation study. A glossary of terms commonly employed in simulation research is included at the end of the chapter.

## Introduction

Initial attempts to understand the mechanics of a sports skill usually involve a subjective evaluation of the performance by a trained observer. Seldom, however, does this type of qualitative analysis furnish sufficiently accurate information for research purposes. To investigate the temporal, kinematic and kinetic factors adequately, electronic and/or photo-instrumentation must be called into play. Such scientific approaches to the study of the mechanical characteristics of human motion have gained wide acceptance and continue to provide much needed descriptive data. Although there still remains a great deal to be learned at the experimental level, some investigators have ventured a step further into the realm of computer simulation of biomechanical systems. It is anticipated that simulation, in conjunction with the traditional experimental methods, will provide a deeper understanding of human motion.

Computer simulation has been used extensively in engineering, business and medical research but has only recently been applied to systems in sport. In the present context, the term system may encompass the body of a gymnast, represent a tennis player and his racquet or be restricted to the recovery leg of a

---

* The writer gratefully acknowledges the work of Michael Bracegirdle in preparing the figures for this chapter.

sprinter. It may even refer to a sports implement. A computer model is a mathematical representation of the system in which the equations defining its components and their interactions are written in a form appropriate for computer analysis. The actual process of studying the behaviour of systems under rigidly controlled conditions using the computer model is termed simulation.

Like any other research technique, computer simulation has both advantages and limitations. On the positive side, it is ideally suited to cases which involve extensive mathematical calculations. The computer can perform these operations quickly and accurately and in greater volume than would be humanly possible. Its most important feature, however, is the ability to provide carefully controlled conditions under which a sports skill can be studied. Physical education teachers and coaches appreciate the problems encountered in attempting to have an athlete repeat all aspects of a performance exactly. It is even more difficult to have a student alter a skill in some prescribed manner without also introducing additional changes. A computer model, on the other hand, will obey instructions precisely. It may, therefore, provide useful information in answer to such questions as, 'How would the performance be altered if the take-off angle were increased in the long jump? . . . if more force were applied to the discus? . . . if the angular velocity of the recovery leg in running were increased? . . . if a longer but lighter club were used in a golf drive?' and numerous others. A computer model permits the influence of a single variable or any desired combination of variables to be investigated.

The term simulation means 'to feign', 'give a false appearance of', 'look or act like'. As these definitions suggest, the simulation is merely a representation of the actual performance just as the computer model is a prototype of the real system. Because the human body and its motion are extremely complex, a considerable number of simplifying assumptions must be introduced into any model used to simulate performance in sport. It must be acknowledged that all aspects of a particular system cannot be represented with complete accuracy. Simplicity in a model is also a desirable attribute. Since it is impossible to maximize both accuracy and simplicity in a simulation study, the investigator must attempt to identify some optimum combination of the two. The artificial nature of a simulation model can be considered its greatest limitation.

## Simulation Models

Simulation models may be classified as being either stochastic or deterministic. Stochastic models include one or more relationships which are based upon the laws of chance. Simulation of the strategies and outcomes of baseball and soccer games fall into this category. Deterministic models, on the other hand, do not depend upon probability functions. They consist of exact relationships so that the same results will always be obtained under identical input conditions. These models are particularly well suited for the mechanical analysis of sports skills. Although both types are found in current research, the majority of biomechanical studies tend to be deterministic.

## Stochastic Simulations

In team games like ice hockey, baseball, football and soccer, it has been customary to keep elaborate statistics. This information is invaluable in the simulation of competitive situations in these sports. Lindsey (1959, 1961, 1963) used such data from the American, National and International Baseball Leagues to investigate game strategy, batting patterns and the progress of the score throughout the innings. He was able to provide statistical evidence to support the contention that left handed batters have a greater probability of obtaining a hit off right handed pitchers than do right handed batters and vice versa. He also showed that a temporary 'slump' in batting might be attributed to the laws of chance rather than to an actual decrease in skill level. Utilizing extensive data from a large number of major league games, Lindsey (1963) studied the relationship between the score in a particular inning and the probability of winning the game; the effectiveness of a given situation in producing runs; the advisability of giving intentional walks; as well as the statistical implications of double plays, base stealing and sacrifice hits. These examples illustrate the importance of having sufficient descriptive data on the system components and their interactions in order to obtain the best results from simulation studies. This is especially true with stochastic models where the probability functions must be based on a large representative sample if they are to provide realistic inferences.

Recently, Garrett et al. (1973) reported on a stochastic model used in the simulation of American football games. An aspiring coach could use such a computer program to advantage in gaining experience in strategy. Upon the presentation of a specific set of conditions describing a game situation, he could respond by designating an offensive or defensive play which he felt would be effective. The probability of such a play's being successful would then be assessed by the computer using data from a large number of previous football games. Feedback on the result of the proposed strategy would be immediate, permitting the user to benefit from a great deal of coaching practice in a short period of time without requiring an actual game situation.

## Deterministic Simulations

Two distinct types of deterministic biomechanical models have emerged to aid in the study of human mechanics. The first, referred to as external models, are those which treat the athlete as a linked system, quasi-rigid body or even as a particle but consider only external forces acting upon the system. Baumann's (1973) tobogganing model and Miller's (1970) diving simulation exemplify this approach. Others, termed internal, such as those of Chaffin (1969) and Beckett and Chang (1968) deal with muscle forces and torques at the joints as well as with the external influences. These mathematical representations consider individual segments or groups of segments rather than the body as a whole. When the system includes all the body links acting together, the internal muscle and joint forces cancel one another and, therefore, do not appear in the analysis. A brief description of a number of the existing external and internal models of the mechanics of human motion will help to illustrate the kind of simulation research presently being undertaken.

Golf, a popular recreational and competitive sport has among its following, several mathematicians, engineers and physicists. Their natural fascination with the mechanical aspects of golf has grown from personal involvement in, and at times, perhaps frustration with the sport. Many of the recent investigations, including efforts to mathematically model the swing, have been conducted by such individuals. Williams (1967) attempted to find what forces must be exerted by a player to produce a specified motion of the golf club. His model divided the downswing into two phases. The first comprised the portion in which the arms, hands and club moved as a single rigid unit about the fixed axis of rotation. The second part dealt with the subsequent uncocking of the wrists which continued until impact with the ball. Williams assumed that the movements of the clubshaft and the arms were confined to a single plane and that, in the second stage, the arms maintained a constant angular velocity. Although their methods of analysis were somewhat different, both Cochran & Stobbs (1968) and Jorgensen (1970) also favoured the use of a planar double pendulum model (Figure 1) to investigate the intricacies of the downswing including the illusive 'timing' factor for the uncocking of the wrists.

It is commonly recognized that the mass centre of a projectile follows a characteristic parabolic flight path provided that it is not significantly influenced by any external force other than the pull of gravity. When such a projectile is an athlete performing a dive from a springboard, however, it is also important to know the movements of the trunk and limbs with respect to the spinning axis through the mass centre of the body. Miller (1971) developed a mathematical model which completely defined the position and orientation of the body during the flight portion of a dive. The path of the mass centre was predicted from Newton's laws of particle motion under the assumption of negligible air resistance. A mathematical prototype of the human body previously developed by Hanavan (1964) was modified to provide a four link representation of the diver which included head-trunk, legs, right arm and left arm segments (Figure 2). Because of these simplifications in body structure, the model was restricted to the study of nontwisting dives performed in the pike and layout positions.

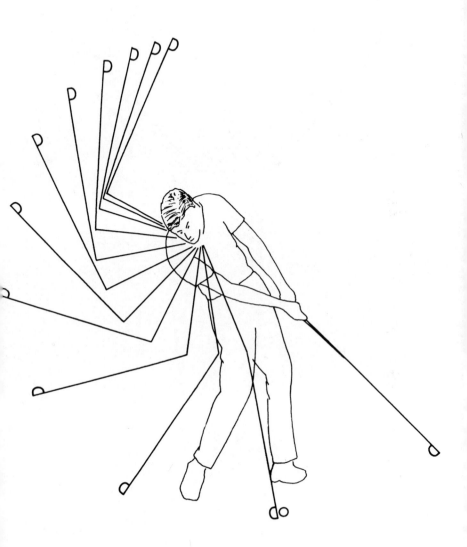

*Fig. 1. Double Pendulum Model of the Golf Swing. (Cochran & Stobbs 1968)*

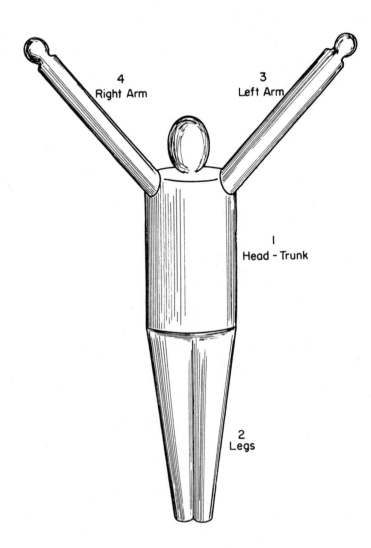

*Fig. 2. Four Link Diving Model. (Miller 1971)*

The rotational components of the trunk and limbs were prescribed by employing the principles of angular momentum conservation. This deterministic computer model was designed to investigate how the total performance of the dive would be influenced by altering such factors as the body proportions of the diver, initial conditions at the take-off and limb movements. Computer output for the simulated dive included a numerical description of the angular displacements and velocities of the body segments and the mass centre location as well as a three dimensional graphics display of the performance.

A simplified mathematical model was constructed by Seireg & Baz (1971) to analyze the mechanics of swimming. In the model, the body of the swimmer was represented by five rigid segments; the trunk-head, two arms and two legs. Equations of motion, utilizing force-mass-acceleration principles, took into account the external forces acting upon the system. These included the body weight and buoyant force with vertical lines of action as well as the horizontal and vertical components of drag resistance, and the combined hydrodynamic and inertial forces acting upon the stretched limbs (Figure 3). Using the example

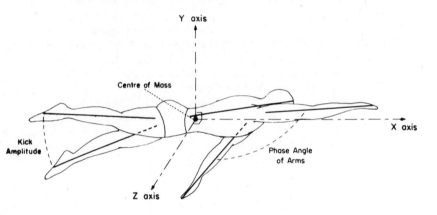

*Fig. 3. Five Segment Swimming Model. (Seireg & Baz 1971)*

of the front crawl stroke, Seireg & Baz assumed that the legs always moved opposite one another and that the resultant thrust from the legs was dependent upon the amplitude and frequency of the kick. The resultant of the propulsive and lift force components generated by the arms was considered dependent upon the phase angle between the arms and the period of the arm cycle. Substitution of the appropriate experimental values into the equations of the model permitted the prediction of the horizontal displacement and velocity of the five segment representation of the swimmer under the specified input conditions as well as its vertical displacement and rotation about the z axis.

A more extensive computer model to analyze swimming strokes was recently reported by Gallenstein & Huston (1973). These investigators employed Hanavan's (1964) 15 segment mathematical representation of the human body to study the flutter and breaststroke kicks as well as the breaststroke itself. Their theoretical analysis was based upon equations of motion which included drag and inertial forces. Input to the model consisted of the anthropometric characteristics of Hanavan's Air Force Mean Man, external forces, and selected time histories of the 28 internal limb angles which defined the swimmer's motion. The output indicated the resulting linear and angular orientations of the chest segment. The simulation model showed the breaststroke kick to be more effective than a bent knee flutter kick while the latter was superior to a straight leg action. Simulation also revealed that the velocity achieved in the breaststroke was slightly less than the sum of the velocities generated by separate arm and leg motions. The writers attributed this to increased profile drag as a result of the combined motion and the higher velocity of the complete stroke.

In a series of articles, Ramey (1970, 1972, 1973) has indicated the potential of the simulation technique for investigating long jump performance. By focusing on the take-off, he was able to demonstrate the importance of rapid extension of the thrusting leg in accelerating the athlete upward. Subsequently, he developed a nine segment planar model of the body based upon the principles of angular momentum conservation. This model was used to simulate the sail, hang and hitchkick styles of long jumping and to show the relative angular momentum required by each of these flight techniques.

In the realm of winter sports, Baumann (1973) developed an external mathematical model of the mechanical factors influencing tobogganing. A second order nonlinear differential equation of motion included such variables as the friction coefficients; air resistance; weight of the toboggan and of the athlete; initial velocity; and the length, slope and average radii of the various sections of the course. Descriptive data defining these variables were obtained at the World Tobogganing Championships held in West Germany in 1970. When these data were used in the model, good agreement was found between the simulated and actual time required to complete the course.

One of the forerunners of contemporary internal models of a deterministic nature was developed by Pearson, McGinley & Butzel (1963). It was designed to study joint forces and muscle torques of upper extremity motions in a sagittal plane. For the investigation, the physical system was conceived as two solid rigid segments representing the upper arm and forearm-hand. The joint between the two links was frictionless and pinned. Extension of this type of model to permit the general analysis of any three segment planar motion was made by Plagenhoef (1971). Dillman (1971) also developed equations of motion to relate both internal and external forces to a three link motion, specifically the recovery leg (thigh, lower leg and foot) in sprint running. From his mathematical model, Dillman was able to predict the resultant moment of force produced by all the muscles acting upon a particular segment and thus determine the dominant muscle groups during the swing of the recovery leg.

A seven link sagittal plane model of the human body was designed by Chaffin (1969; Chaffin & Baker 1970) to investiage the maximum weight an individual was capable of lifting in specified positions (Figure 4). The maximum voluntary torques at the major articulations of the body were estimated from tests of static strength. Biomechanical properties of the segments were also used in the model. A static lifting position was simulated and a small external force applied to the hands to represent the resistance of an object being lifted. The resulting torques generated at each of the major joints were calculated and compared with their respective limiting values. The external force at the hands

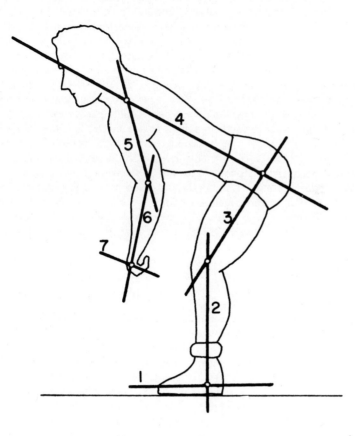

*Fig. 4. Seven Segment Lifting Model. (Chaffin 1969)*

was then increased and the calculations repeated until one of the torques reached or exceeded its limit. When this occurred, the computer printed out the weight being lifted, the torques produced at the joint and the corresponding predictions of their maximum values. Validation of the model showed it to be predicting consistently that an individual was capable of lifting greater loads then he demonstrated in practice. In an attempt to correct this, estimates of compression forces upon the lumbo-sacral disc were introduced. The original trunk-head segment was, therefore, divided into two links, the pelvis and the spine. This modification permitted unbiased estimates of lifting strength to be made.

Using the model just described, Quigley & Chaffin (1971) investigated the heel lift forces, ankle torques and gastrocnemius tensions in various downhill skiing positions. They found that the upward force exerted upon the heel binding showed greater increases in an erect straight running position than in a crouch as the steepness of the skiing slope increased. Thus, much larger torques were produced at the ankle in the erect posture. These results confirm the mechanical soundness of the skier's tendency to adopt a more pronounced crouch position on the steeper hills. Quigley & Chaffin were also able to demonstrate that the 'average' woman skier, although generating smaller absolute forces and torques than her male counterpart, expends a greater proportion of her total strength in skiing. This research illustrates that a great deal can be learned about the behaviour of a system through mathematical modelling even though a considerable number of simplifications have to be incorporated into the simulation. In this instance, the computerized bio-mechanical model represented the body as a seven link system and was limited to the analysis of symmetric static positions or constant velocity motions in a single plane. To further reduce the complexity of the equations, the influences of uneven ground, changes in direction, air and frictional resistance were omitted.

Significant interest has been expressed in human locomotion and, as a result, considerable research has been directed toward gaining a more complete understanding of the mechanics of this fundamental skill. The aspects of normal running gait are of particular concern to the physical educator just as a typical walking patterns are to those in rehabilitation medicine. Designers of artificial limbs must also be knowledgeable in this area. In addition to other research techniques, several mathematical models have been developed to study the various facets of locomotion (Nubar & Contini 1961; Beckett & Chang 1968; Chen & Huang 1970; Dillman 1971; Chow & Jacobson 1971; 1972). Although normal gait appears to be a simple skill, in mechanical terms it is extremely complex. The necessary equations of motion contain numerous variables including the masses, centres of mass and moments of inertia of each of the body segments in the model as well as their positions, displacements and velocities as functions of time; the moments of force at the joint which result from muscle action; and the reaction forces at the joints and other points of external support. In most cases, this means that the number of unknowns exceeds the number of equations. Therefore, further simplifications must be introduced if all the unknowns are to be completely defined. To accomplish this, Aubar & Contini (1961) and Beckett & Chang (1968) employed the principle of minimum energy. This concept is based upon the assumption that a normal person, performing well practiced and almost involuntary motor actions such as walking, will automatically adjust his movements so that he expends a minimum amount of energy. Through the application of this special condition, which involves extensive mathematical calculations, it is possible to solve the equations of motion governing certain aspects of walking.

The principle of minimum energy, which implies that a minimum level of muscular effort is used to satisfy the requirements of a task, appears to be a reasonable assumption for posture and walking. It is debatable whether it can also be applied to the performance of sports skills. In comparing the inefficient thrashing of a beginning swimmer with the smooth and seemingly effortless patterns of motion of the Olympic champion, it is apparent that the absence of extraneous movements in the skilled athlete is indicative of a much lower energy expenditure for a given task. Thus, for highly skilled performers, the assumption of minimum energy may be valid. These athletes have repeated their sports movement so often that it has evolved into an efficient action which is almost as automatic as the gait of an average individual.

Modern control theory, however, is not restricted to concepts of minimum energy. The optimization may well be related to such parameters as power, mechanical work or time. In this connection, Hatze (1973) has begun to develop a mathematical model to predict the optimum mechanical performance components of a specific type of motion for a given individual under set environmental conditions. This type of approach would have important coaching implications. If successful, it would mean that an athlete could achieve his maximum performance in a much shorter period of time than is commonly the case under trial and error conditions. It should be realized, however, that the construction of such a model is an enormous undertaking fraught with countless theoretical, technical and practical problems.

The rapid growth of simulation studies in biomechanics since 1968 has been impressive. From the examples cited, it can be appreciated that deterministic mathematical models have been constructed to analyze a variety of sports. Throughout the course of the discussion, certain common denominators may have become apparent. Only extremely simplified and idealized versions of real life systems have been included in the models. This is exemplified by the portrayal of the human body as a small number of rigid segments and the restriction of many of the analyses to a single plane of motion. Some of the prototypes are still in the initial or exploratory stages. Further work and modification will increase their value for predicting performances under specified conditions. Nevertheless, the disciplined quantitative approach to th analysis required in the construction of a simulation model, in itself, provide valuable insights into the mechanics of the biomechanical system.

## Steps in Computer Simulation Research

The examples of computer simulation studies just described indicate th applications and potential of this research technique. Despite the apparen diversity of the models, similar procedures were followed in their constructio and in the subsequent simulation of the particular system. For the purpose o discussion, these have been arbitrarily divided into *six* steps: (1) definition of th problem; (2) construction of the mathematical model; (3) computerization; (4 validation; (5) determination of input data; and, ultimately (6) simulation of th system to study its behaviour under specified conditions. It is hoped that th following detailed consideration of each of these steps will aid in th understanding of simulation research and will provide guidelines for thos attempting to use the technique.

## Definition of the Problem

The initial phase in planning any research project is to identify and define th problem to be studied, set limits upon the scope of the investigation and develo a sound frame of reference which will guide the subsequent stages of th research. Many factors must be considered and a number of questions answered What is the purpose of the study? How will the results be used? What level o accuracy is required? Upon the basis of the responses, the most appropriat experimental design and instrumentation must be selected.

Although computer simulation will not be a suitable technique for a research problems, it should be seriously considered in studying those which ar amenable to quantitative analysis. Such a technique has distinct advantage where extensive mathematical calculations are required. For example, compute simulation may be used to gain a deeper insight into the operation of a system to study system behaviour under rigidly controlled conditions and, ultimately to predict the reaction of the system and its components to specified situations

## Construction of the Mathematical Model

The most important and yet most difficult step in simulation research is the construction of a valid mathematical model to represent the system, its components and their interactions. This is the key to a successful study equations must be derived which portray the essential aspects of the system with acceptable accuracy and, yet, incorporate a sufficient number of simplifying assumptions so that the model does not become too complex.

The information summarized in Table 1 may provide some guidance in selecting the type of mechanical analysis which best suits the objectives of the simulation. Using Newtonian mechanics, the system can be classified as either static or dynamic. Chaffin's (1969) model for investigating the forces and torques at the major articulations of the body during lifting tasks is an example of a simulation utilizing the principles of statics. In the case of dynamics, further subdivision should be made into kinematics (the time-geometry of motion without reference to the underlying forces) and kinetics (the investigation of the influence of forces upon the system). Equations of motion for kinetic analysis are generally derived by utilizing the force-mass-acceleration, work-energy or impulse-momentum approaches depending upon whether the forces are analyzed at an instant, over a distance or during a time period.

Table 1

*Approaches to the Construction of Mathematical Models*

NEWTONIAN MECHANICS

| | |
|---|---|
| Statics | Equilibrium and nonaccelerated motion |
| Dynamics | Accelerated motion |
|   Kinematics | Time-geometry of motion |
|   Kinetics | Study of forces analyzed: |
|     Force-mass-acceleration | - at an instant |
|     Work-energy | - over a distance |
|     Impulse-momentum | - during impact or over a time period |

LAGRANGIAN MECHANICS             Most suitable for multi-body problems

*Force-Mass-Acceleration.* Because both internal and external forces fluctuate considerably during the course of any human motion, it is important to investigate their changes in magnitude and direction at successive points in time. The force-mass-acceleration approach, based upon an instantaneous analysis of forces, is one of the best means of analyzing such a situation. In the two dimensional or coplanar case, equations of motion are derived by summing all the forces or force components in a given direction and setting them equal to the product of the mass and the acceleration of the mass centre. Thus,

$$\Sigma F_x = ma_x \quad \text{and} \quad \Sigma F_y = ma_y.$$

The torques or moments of force about a specific axis are also summed. The equation $\Sigma M_o = I_o \alpha$ represents a special case where o is an axis through the mass

centre or a fixed point; $I_O$ is the moment of inertia with respect to an ax
through o; and $\alpha$ is the angular acceleration of the body. In the thre
dimensional case, the moment equations are more complex.

When constructing models concerned with the internal muscle and join
forces as well as the external influences, it is customary to study the system b
parts. Thus, in Dillman's (1971) model of the recovery leg in sprint running, th
foot was analyzed first (Figure 5), then the lower leg and ultimately the thigh i

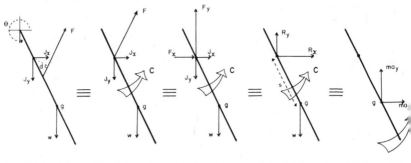

a) Original free body
   diagram of the foot.

b) Replacing resultant
   muscle force with
   an equivalent force
   and a couple.

c) Dividing F into
   horizontal and
   vertical components.

d) Adjusted free body
   diagram of the foot.

e) Resultant - force
   diagram of the
   foot.

### KEY TO SYMBOLS

$J_x$ $J_y$   Components of joint reaction forces.

W, m   Segment weight and mass.

$F(F_x F_y)$ Resultant muscle force.

d        Moment arm of F with respect to
         the ankle.

θ        Angle of foot with horizontal.

C        Resultant muscular couple or torque   $C = F \times d$.

s        Distance from ankle joint to mass centre.

$R_x$ $R_y$, Components of resultant muscle-joint reaction force

$a_x$ $a_y$, Components of mass centre acceleration.

α        Angular acceleration of the foot.

$I_g$    Segment moment of inertia with respect to the
         mass centre (g).

### THE EQUATIONS OF MOTION OF THE FOOT

Sum of horizontal forces   $R_x = m \times a_x$       Sum of vertical forces   $R_y - W = m \times a_y$

Sum of moments about the ankle joint   $C - W \times S \times \cos\theta = I_g \times \alpha - m \times a_x \times S \times \sin\theta + m \times a_y \times S \times c$

*Fig. 5. Force — Mass — Acceleration Approach. (Dillman 1971)*

order to estimate resultant muscular torques. Such a sequential treatment i
necessary to reduce the unknowns in the equations of motion. Since the precis
locations of muscle attachments cannot be ascertained accurately, it i
exceedingly difficult, if not impossible, to identify the magnitudes and

directions of individual muscle forces. It is feasible, however, to consider their vector sum, which is referred to as the resultant muscle force F. For the purpose of mechanical analysis, F may be replaced by a force of equal magnitude and direction acting through the joint and a couple or torque C which is equivalent to the moments of all the original muscle forces. If moments are then taken about the joint, the number of unknowns in the three equations of motion is reduced to the resultant muscle couple C and two orthogonal force components RX and RY with lines of action through the joint. The force components represent the algebraic sum of the joint reaction and translated muscle forces. Since the resultant force and torque at the proximal joint of one segment are equal in magnitude and opposite in direction to the corresponding resultant force and torque at the distal joint of the adjoining segment, their values may be substituted into the appropriate equations of motion as the analysis proceeds sequentially from segment to segment.

The type of model employed by Dillman (1971) assumes that the muscles involved cross only one joint or that the error introduced by disregarding two joint muscles can be neglected. It is appropriate for estimating resultant muscular torque patterns at the major articulations. Although the model cannot identify the contribution of a specific muscle, reasonable predictions may be made about the pattern of dominant muscle group activity during the performance of a skill. From a practical standpoint, this is undoubtedly of greater importance since muscles seldom act independently.

*Impulse-Momentum.* The impulse-momentum approach to kinetic analysis is best suited for biomechanical problems in which linear or angular motion changes over a specified time interval. A special case occurs when angular momentum is conserved as in the free fall portion of tumbling, diving, trampolining, dance, figure skating and jumping. In these examples, air resistance is considered negligible and the total angular momentum with respect to an axis through the mass centre of the body remains unchanged during the unsupported phase of the skill. Although this considerably simplifies the construction of the equations of motion of a simulation model, they are still sufficiently complex and lengthy to require the services of a computer.

The angular momentum relationship for an n-link system in free fall may be expressed as:

$$_H S/CS = \text{A Constant}$$
$$= {}_H B1/C1 + {}_H B2/C2 + {}_H B3/C3 + \ldots + {}_H Bn/Cn +$$
$${}_H C1/CS + {}_H C2/CS + {}_H C3/CS + \ldots + {}_H Cn/CS$$

where $H$ is the symbol for angular momentum; B1, ... Bn represent the n interconnected rigid bodies or segments comprising the system; C1, ... Cn are the mass centres of the n segments; S indicates the system as a whole; CS is the mass centre of the system; and / means 'with respect to' (Smith & Kane 1967 Miller 1970). Thus, $H^{S/CS}$ is the angular momentum of the system with respect to its mass centre. On the right hand side of the equation, the $H^{Bi/Ci}$ terms represent the angular momentum $I\omega$ of each segment about its own centre of mass. I is the principal inertia tensor of the segment and $\omega$, the segment angular velocity. The remaining terms $H^{Ci/CS}$ are the moments of momentum of the segmental mass centres about the system mass centre. Each is expressed as the cross product:

$$Ri \times mi \frac{dRi}{dt}$$

where i = 1,n indicates the number of a particular segment; $Ri$ is the position vector joining the segmental mass centre with the centre of mass of the system mi is the segmental mass; and $\frac{dRi}{dt}$ is the time rate of change of $Ri$ or the velocity of the segmental mass centre with reference to the system mass centre.

This angular momentum relationship requires several rather extensive calculations. Since the location of the mass centre of the human body is influenced by the position of the segments, it must be determined repeatedly throughout the motion. In addition, all vectors relating to individual segments must be transformed so that they are compatible with a single reference frame which is common to the whole system. Finally, it is customary to express the angular momentum vector in terms of its components along the three mutually perpendicular axes of the coordinate reference frame.

*Energy Analysis.* A somewhat different analysis of a biomechanical system incorporates the principles of work and energy. The equations of motion relate the work performed by the forces acting during a specified displacement to the resulting change in the kinetic energy. To date, however, this type of analysis has been used relatively little in simulation models (Garrett et al 1971).

If a multi-link system is being investigated, it may be of advantage to apply Lagrangian mechanics to develop the differential equations of motion. This method deals with kinetic and potential energy, utilizes generalized cordinates to define the position of the system and requires expressions of velocity rather than acceleration. It derives as many equations as there are degrees of freedom in the system. Jorgensen (1970) employed this technique to analyze the swing of a golf club. Although the Lagrangian approach generates the necessary mathematical equations, it does not guarantee their solution. In addition, these equations often lack the physical significance characteristic of those developed from Newtonian principles.

*Mathematical Models of the Body.* In many biomechanical models, the system under investigation is the athlete himself. Since it is impossible to represent the intricacies of the human body with complete accuracy, it has become common practice to treat man as a particle, quasi-rigid body or linked system depending upon the objectives of the investigation. Thus, in simulating the distance covered by a long jumper, it might be sufficient to consider the displacement of his mass centre. In other instances, the athlete is portrayed as a quasi-rigid body. This implies that, although his segments are capable of individual movement, they remain at rest with respect to one another and the whole body moves as if it were a single rigid unit. Such would be the case of a diver spinning in a tuck or a gymnast maintaining a stretched position during a dismount. A more realistic (and involved) approach recognizes individual movement of the segments and treats the human body as a linked system. Unfortunately, there is a considerable increase in the complexity of the equations as the number of body segments increases. For this reason, a model used to study nontwisting pike and layout dives (Miller 1971) was restricted to four segments. Similarly, a seven link coplanar system was employed to investigate the forces and torques generated in various lifting tasks (Chaffin 1969). As a general rule, it is advisable to reduce the number of segments in the model of the human body to the absolute minimum necessary to accomplish the objectives of the simulation.

In studies concerned with the forces influencing human movement, the model must include information on the biomechanical properties of the body, namely segmental lengths, masses, centres of mass and moments of inertia. Several mathematical representations of the human body have evolved in conjunction with the American space program. They were originally intended for use in predicting the movements of astronauts in free fall and under conditions of reduced gravity. The early models (Kulwicki & Schlei 1962; Whitsett 1963) were rather crude but later versions were gradually refined to provide a more realistic quantitative portrayal of the human body (Hanavan 1964; Tieber & Lindemuth 1965). The majority of these and similar models represent the human body as a linked system of rigid segments of common geometric shape and homogeneous composition joined by hinged, frictionless articulations. Hands and feet are considered single segments. Changes in volume caused by blood flow and tissue deformation are neglected. Segmental mass distribution is expressed as a function of total body mass and is derived from regression equations based upon cadaver data. Mass centres and moments of inertia are determined mathematically using the geometric configurations of the segments. These assumptions make it possible to construct a mathematical model of the human body which is suitable for programming on a computer.

One of the most widely used mathematical representations of the body is the 15 segment model developed by Hanavan (1964) (Figure 6). Although it was originally designed as a computer program to calculate the inertial properties of the total body in specific positions, parts of the program may be utilized to obtain lengths, masses, mass centre locations and principal moments of inertia of the 15 segments. Twenty-five anthropometric measurements of the subject

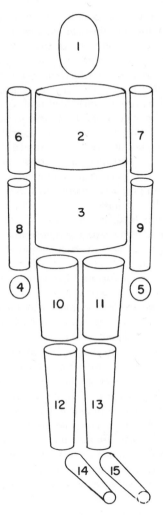

*Fig. 6. The Hanavan Model. (Hanavan 1964)*

including segment lengths, circumferences and body weight are used to specify
the dimensions of the segments and to account for differences in physique.

The main weakness of existing mathematical models of the human body is
their dependence upon extremely small samples of adult male cadavers for data
on segmental mass distribution. Therefore, their scope of inference cannot be
extended beyond the adult male population without some reservations. Hanavan

used Barter's (1957) regression equations which statistically combined the results of Braune and Fischer (1889), Fischer (1906) and Dempster (1955) to increase the sample size to 12. In a recent investigation, Clauser *et al.* (1969) studied the mass proportions of 13 male cadavers. It is anticipated that this information will be incorporated into future models. Thus the necessity to continually update mathematical representations of the human body with current biomechanical data becomes apparent. At present, there is a particularly acute need for more information on the segmental parameters of women and children.

## Computerization

While it is possible to carry out mathematical simulations without the services of a high speed electronic computer, the scope of the study and its potential are greatly increased when this type of instrumentation is employed. The computer, a device capable of performing simple arithmetic and logic operations at remarkable speeds, is available in several different forms. The analog computer processes data of a continuous nature while the digital version deals with discrete bits of information. The hybrid machine is a combination of the two. Most simulations of human movement have been performed on the large digital computers commonly found in universities and industry. With the increasing popularity and widespread use of minicomputers and electronic programmable calculators, however, these machines will undoubtedly play an augmented role in simulation research in the future. At present, their relatively small information storage capacity or 'memory' limits their application to the smaller and less complicated simulation models.

Any one of several different languages may be used to program the equations of a simulation model for solution on a digital computer. The language chosen must be compatible with the particular computer employed in the study. The choice also depends upon the knowledge of the investigator or the individual doing the programming. Certain rules of syntax must be observed although, in most cases, an equation expressed in computer language closely resembles its original form. Irrespective of the machine or language employed, several general suggestions can be made regarding the computerization of the simulation model.

It is extremely important to maintain complete documentation on the computer program. A list should be kept of all the variables in the model such as leg length, arm mass, body weight, specific displacements, velocities and accelerations including their units of measurement and the names used to represent them in the program. If variable names are employed, they should be mnemonic so that they can be more readily recognized. For example, VEL is more indicative of velocity than a designation such as B or F. Similarly, ARML might be used to refer to arm length and CG to centre of gravity. Rules for the naming of variables are governed by the particular computer language. Where possible, generous use should be made of comments throughout the program. Comments are statements which are not executed by the computer but which provide useful reminders to the programmer. They may indicate the date of the latest revision of the model, titles for subsections of the program, and rationale for the inclusion of certain calculations. When cards are used as the input medium for the computer, they should include information which will identify the particular program for which they are intended. This becomes even more important with the accumulation of several different programs. Cards should contain sequence numbers which indicate their proper order in the deck. At least one duplicate copy of the computer program should be kept as insurance against loss of the original.

The results generated by the computer may or may not be correct. The fact that the answers appear in the form of computer output does not guarantee their infallibility. Therefore, a system of verification must be incorporated throughout all stages of the model construction and computerization. Periodic checks of the equations should be made to ensure that there is consistency in the units of measurement. Care must be taken to avoid errors in transcription. When programming the mathematical model, provision should be made to print out the results at a number of intermediate stages in the calculations to ensure that logical answers are being obtained. The information which was originally fed into the program should also be printed. Hand calculations should be performed to verify the results during initial runs of the program. Once the accuracy of the computer model has been established, a set of test data and the output it generates should be kept on file for future use.

The characteristic output from computer programs is numerical. The programmer can specify the information and results he wishes printed as well as the format in which they are to be presented. It is customary to provide a time history of the variables during the course of the simulation. In the case of total body movement, this could include the linear and angular displacements, velocities and accelerations of the limbs at .01 second intervals throughout the specified action.

The output medium of computer graphics may also be used to great advantage in displaying simulation results in pictorial form. Not only can graphs be generated by the computer but two and three dimensional diagrams can be drawn (Figure 7). To produce this form of computer output, graphics programs must be written. If the human body is to be the basic display unit, the computer must be instructed how to draw it. In most systems, this involves specifying a sequence of coordinate reference points to guide the pen of a plotting machine or the light beam of a cathode ray tube. Since the computer is only capable of drawing straight lines, curves are usually approximated by a series of very short straight line segments. Information defining the translation and rotation of the body segments resulting from the simulation are applied to the basic graphic

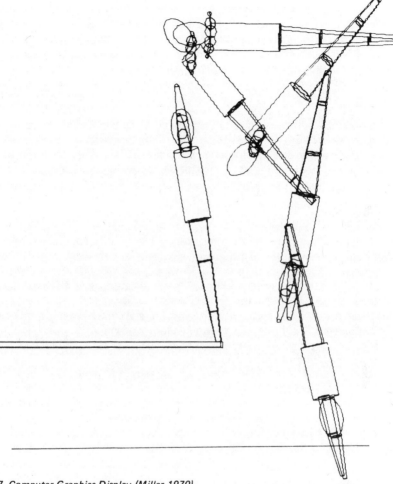

*Fig. 7. Computer Graphics Display (Miller 1970)*

representation of the body. It is then appropriately displayed on paper as
specified number of distinct images or in apparent continuous motion on the
screen of a cathode ray oscilloscope.

## Validation of the Model

The validity of the computer model must now be assessed in the light of the original objectives of the simulation. Are the assumptions tenable? Have the various simplifications introduced too much error into the results? And, most important, are the equations of motion correct? Answers to these and other pertinent questions are usually sought by comparing the computer's prediction of the behaviour of the system under a particular set of circumstances (input conditions) with the results obtained experimentally using high speed cameras, force transducers or other suitable instrumentation. While perfect agreement between the two is a rather idealistic goal, good correspondence should be expected. It must be realized, however, that the experimental estimates of the criterion may not be completely accurate but in all probability possess a certain inherent error. This factor has to be taken into consideration when making the final decision on the computer model's capability of providing sufficiently accurate results to fulfil the objectives of the simulation study.

In the diving model (Miller 1970), validation was accomplished by comparing the computer output with the performance recorded on 16 mm film. The input variables (take-off conditions, total angular momentum and limb motions) obtained cinematographically were used by the computer to predict the location and orientation of the diver after leaving the springboard. Subsequent film analysis of the flight of the dive provided experimental evidence which supported the output of the simulation model.

In some instances, validation results may indicate that further modifications of the model are required. As' mentioned earlier, Chaffin & Baker (1970) discovered that their original seven segment model overestimated an individual's lifting ability. To bring the experimental and computer results into better agreement, approximations of the compression forces at the lumbo-sacral disc were introduced into the model.

Thus, the validation procedure is an extremely important step in the simulation method of research. It not only provides information on the authenticity of the equations in the model but may also result in the detection of errors in their derivation or transcription which have previously gone unnoticed. The confidence with which prediction of performance can be made rests upon this stage in the development of the computer simulation model.


## Determination of Input Values

Each computer model requires certain input data from which calculations and predictions can be made. Some programs use anthropometric measurements of subjects to define the biomechanical properties of the body segments (Hanavan 1964). Others utilize information on muscle torques which can be generated at the major articulations (Chaffin 1969). External forces of friction and air resistance may be of concern (Baumann 1973). Such information supplies the initial conditions and boundary values which set limits upon the performance of biomechanical systems. Before a realistic simulation of a given model can be accomplished, the user must have good estimates of the normal ranges of these variables. Thus, the velocity of a sprinter might be estimated between 25 and 35 feet per second. A value of 50 feet per second would be unreasonable and would not yield representative results if used as input for computer model. In most cases, however, there is a dearth of 'normal' quantitative data describing performance in sport. For example, what is the angular momentum required for a 3 1/2 somersault in the tuck position? What is the angular velocity—time relationship of the takeoff leg in the long jump? What is the pattern of the impulse from the ground exerted on a volleyball player going up for a spike? Only carefully conducted descriptive studies can provide such information. And, until it is available in sufficient quantity and quality, simulation studies will not achieve their fullest potential.

## Simulation

Once a valid model has been developed and adequate descriptive data are available for input, the actual simulation of the system under various conditions can begin. The influence of single variables upon the performance should be studied first. Later the interactions of two or more variables can be examined. Results of the initial simulations will undoubtedly suggest other avenues of investigation. When the system has been studied as completely as desired with the existing computer model, the next step may be to construct a more elaborate mathematical representation of the particular biomechanical system which is capable of providing increased insight into its behaviour.

## Example of the Computer Simulation of a Simple System

While computerized models of human motion tend to be rather complex, the basic concepts of this type of research may be illustrated with comparatively simple example of the simulation of the flight of a shot after it leaves the athlete's hand. Although the shot is not a complicated system when compared with the human body, similar principles are involved in developing the simulation.

## Definition of the Problem

The purpose of the simulation is to study the effect of the release velocity (magnitude and direction) and the height of release upon the horizontal distance covered by the shot. Therefore, the model is restricted to the flight of the shot which is that portion of its motion occurring between release and contact with the ground. For the purpose of the investigation, the effect of air resistance is disregarded.

## Construction of the Mathematical Model

The shot, represented by its mass centre, is treated as a particle. The equations of motion are derived from the principles of Newtonian mechanics utilizing the force-mass-acceleration approach. In the air, the shot follows a parabolic trajectory the nature of which is determined at the instant of release. The equations ($\Sigma F = MA$), however, apply only to straight line motion. An examination of the free body diagram (Figure 8a), which isolates the system from its surroundings and shows all the external forces acting upon it, indicates that the only force influencing the shot is its weight. The latter is directed vertically downwards. Since air resistance is considered negligible, there is no force to alter the flight of the shot in the horizontal direction (Figure 8b). Thus,

WEIGHT

*Fig. 8a. Free Body Diagram of the Shot in Flight.*

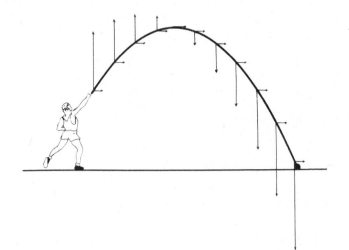

*Fig. 8b. Horizontal and Vertical Velocity Components of the Trajectory of the Shot.*

the horizontal and the vertical have physical significance to the problem being investigated and also provide two orthogonal directions upon which the analysis can be based.

Horizontally,  $\Sigma F_h = MA_h$

$0 = MA_h$

$A_h = 0$

and vertically  $\Sigma F_v = MA_v$

$-W = \dfrac{W}{G} A_v$

$A_v = -G$

where G is the acceleration due to gravity; A is acceleration; M is mass; W is weight; and the subscripts h and v refer to the horizontal and vertical respectively*. Integrating these equations once yields velocity-time relationships:

$$V_h = V_{hi} \qquad (1) \qquad \text{and} \qquad V_v = V_{vi} - GT \qquad (2).$$

Integrating a second time produces displacement-time relationships:

$$S_h = V_{hi} T \qquad (3) \qquad \text{and} \qquad S_v = V_{vi} T - 1/2\, GT^2 + S_{vi} \qquad (4).$$

where S refers to displacement; the subscript i indicates an initial value; and T is the time. These four equations provide the basic mathematical model for the simulation. With specific reference to the shot put:

$V_{hi}$ is the horizontal component of velocity of the shot at release;

$V_{vi}$ is the vertical component of velocity of the shot at release; and

$S_{vi}$ is the height of the shot at release.

These three values must be furnished as input to the model.

Since the vertical component of velocity is zero at the highest point of the trajectory, the time required to reach this point can be calculated using Equation 2. Its height is then determined from Equation 4. Utilizing this information, the time for the shot to reach the ground from the peak of the trajectory is also computed from Equation 4. The total time that the shot is in the air is the sum of the time for it to reach the highest point and the subsequent time to strike the ground. Substitution of the total time, along with the horizontal component of velocity, into Equation 3 yields the horizontal distance covered by the shot under specified input conditions.

---

* The convention of upward being positive and downward being negative has been adopted.

Although the mathematical model is derived from the principles of kinetics, once the equations have been developed the problem is one of kinematics. It is the time-geometry of the motion which is of concern. Knowledge of the magnitudes of the forces involved in the action is not required for the solution of the equations in the model.

## Computerization

The equations of motion are programmed (Figure 9) for solution on a high

```
        $JOB WATFIV      140337.MILLER
        C
        C    PROGRAM TO SIMULATE THE FLIGHT OF A SHOT      FEB. 14, 1972
        C
  1          DIMENSION SHORIZ(21,5),ANG(21),PSI(21),VV(21),VH(21)
  2          DATA G/32.2/, PI/3.14159/
        C
        C    VARY RELEASE ANGLE FROM 30 TO 50 DEGREES IN 1 DEGREE INCREMENTS AND
        C    RESULTANT VELOCITY FROM 26 TO 46 FT/SEC IN 1 FT/SEC INCREMENTS
        C
  3          DO 15 I = 1,21
  4          ANG(I) = I + 29
  5       15 PSI(I) = ANG(I)* (PI/180.)
  6          VR = 25.
  7          DO 30 J = 1,21
  8          VR = VR + 1.
        C
        C    STATEMENTS TO SET UP THE OUTPUT FORMAT
        C
  9          IF((J - (J/2)*2).EQ.0) GO TO 11
 10          PRINT 5
 11        5 FORMAT('1',10X, 'COMPUTER SIMULATION OF THE HORIZONTAL DISTANCE '
             1   'COVERED BY A SHOT',/,19X,'AS A FUNCTION OF VELOCITY AND HEIGHT'
             2   ' OF RELEASE',//,50X,'DISTANCE THROWN AS A FUNCTION OF',/,6X,
             3   'VELOCITY OF RELEASE',33X,'HEIGHT OF RELEASE',//,1X,
             4   'RESULTANT  HORIZONTAL  VERTICAL',6X,'ANGLE',8X,'6',6X,
             5   '6.5',6X,'7',6X,'7.5',6X,'8',/10X,'(FEET/SECOND)',13X,'(DEGREES)
             6   ', 20X,'(FEET)',//)
        C
        C    VARY RELEASE HEIGHT FROM 6 TO 8 FEET IN .5 FT INCREMENTS
        C
 12       11 HT = 5.5
 13          DO 24 K = 1,5
 14          HT = HT + .5
        C
        C    CALCULATE THE HORIZONTAL DISTANCE OF THE PUT
        C
 15          DO 25 I = 1,21
 16          VV(I) = VR*SIN(PSI(I))
 17          VH(I) = VR*COS(PSI(I))
 18          TUP = VV(I)/G
 19          SUP = 1./2.*G*TUP**2
 20          SDOWN = SUP + HT
 21          TDOWN = SQRT(2.*SDOWN/G)
 22          TTOT = TUP + TDOWN
 23       25 SHORIZ(I,K) = VH(I)*TTOT
 24       24 CONTINUE
 25          DO 26 I = 1,21
 26          PRINT 12, VR,VH(I),VV(I),ANG(I),(SHORIZ(I,K),K=1,5)
 27       12 FORMAT(' ',2X,3(F5.2,6X),F7.2,6X,5(F5.2,3X))
 28       27 PRINT 13
 29       13 FORMAT(' ',///)
 30       30 CONTINUE
 31          STOP
 32          END
        $ENTRY
```

*Fig. 9. Computer Model to Simulate the Flight of the Shot.*

speed electronic digital computer. The FORTRAN (formula translation) computer language is chosen for this purpose. Following recommended programming practice, comments (identified by a C at the extreme left of the line) are inserted at appropriate points to clarify the rationale of the calculations. The meaning of the variable names used in the program as well as their units of measurement are recorded for future reference in Table 2. The

Table 2

*Variable Names Employed in the Simulation Program*

| Variable Name | Variable | Units |
|---|---|---|
| ANG | Angle of release with respect to the horizontal | Degrees |
| G | Acceleration due to gravity | Ft/sec/sec |
| HT | Height of the shot at release | Feet |
| PSI | Angle of release with respect to the horizontal | Radians |
| SDOWN | Vertical distance from the highest point in the flight of the shot to the ground | Feet |
| SHORIZ | Horizontal distance covered by the shot as a result of the put | Feet |
| SUP | Vertical distance from release to the highest point in the flight | Feet |
| TDOWN | Time from the highest point in the flight until the shot reaches the ground | Seconds |
| TTOT | Total time that the shot is in flight | Seconds |
| TUP | Time from release until the shot reaches the highest point in the flight | Seconds |
| VH | Horizontal component of the velocity of the shot at release | Ft/sec |
| VR | Resultant velocity of the shot at release | Ft/sec |
| VV | Vertical component of the velocity of the shot at release | Ft/sec |

initial conditions of the shot put, which are specified in the program, may be considered input to the model. The resulting horizontal distance covered by the shot is output by the simulation model.

**Validation**

To test the accuracy of the model, experimental data on the input conditions and the resulting distance achieved in the put are obtained for comparison purposes. Several trials of shot putters are filmed with a high speed motion picture camera, the optical axis of which is aligned at right angles to the plane of the release. An object of known length, such as a surveyor's range pole, is also filmed in this plane to provide the necessary information for converting image dimensions to life size. Timing lights within the camera or a timing display in the photographic field are used to determine the actual frame rate at which the camera is operating. Markers indicating the landing points of the shot permit subsequent measurement of the distances achieved in the various trials.

The films are carefully analyzed on a motion analyzer with the readings being repeated on three separate occasions to provide an index of the experimental error attributable to the film analysis. Coordinates of the centre of the shot are recorded from the frames immediately preceding, at and following release. Release is operationally defined as the last frame in which there is any contact between the athlete and the shot. Coordinates of the ground at the front of the shot put circle are also noted.

The film data are used as input to the equations of the computer model. The simulated horizontal distances achieved as a result of the specified release conditions are then compared with appropriate experimental values. In few instances, do the computer predictions agree exactly with their corresponding measured distances. This may be explained by the fact that the athlete does not release the shot precisely above the edge of the circle. No compensation is provided for this in the mathematical model. Should the program be modified to incorporate this distance factor? Considering the objectives set forth initially, the increased complexity that the proposed modification would introduce does not appear justified in terms of the relatively small improvements in accuracy which it would provide. In addition, the influence of the release velocity and height can be investigated adequately with the original computer model. Other discrepancies between the two sets of results fall well within the limits of experimental error in determining the initial conditions of the shot put cinematographically. Therefore, the computer simulation model is accepted as providing adequate information on the horizontal distance achieved in the shot put.

### Determination of the Input Values

Input to the model consists of three variables: height of release, and magnitude and direction of the velocity at release. These are the initial conditions which influence the subsequent trajectory and thus the distance of the put. To obtain meaningful predictions, realistic estimates of these variables must be fed into the computer. Upon the basis of empirical and some experimental evidence, their approximate ranges may be adequately determined.

The height of release will vary from about six feet for young athletes to around eight feet for top calibre putters. Similarly, considering the maximum distances achieved in world competition at one extreme and those of novice putters at the other, it is estimated that the resultant velocity of the shot at release must vary from 26 to 46 feet per second. The shot is usually released at an angle slightly less than 45 degrees with the horizontal.

## Simulation of the System

To obtain an overview of the influence of the conditions at release upon the subsequent flight of the shot, the release height is varied from six to eight feet in .5 foot intervals, the magnitude of the velocity from 26 to 46 feet per second in one foot per second intervals, and the angle of release from 30 to 50 degrees. Output from the model specified the horizontal and vertical components of the initial velocity as well as the distance of the put (Table 3).

### Table 3

COMPUTER SIMULATION OF THE HORIZONTAL DISTANCE COVERED BY A SHOT
AS A FUNCTION OF VELOCITY AND HEIGHT OF RELEASE

| VELOCITY OF RELEASE | | | | DISTANCE THROWN AS A FUNCTION OF HEIGHT OF RELEASE | | | | |
|---|---|---|---|---|---|---|---|---|
| RESULTANT | HORIZONTAL (FEET/SECOND) | VERTICAL | ANGLE (DEGREES) | 6 | 6.5 | 7 (FEET) | 7.5 | 8 |
| 36.00 | 31.18 | 18.00 | 30.00 | 43.23 | 43.81 | 44.38 | 44.93 | 45.48 |
| 36.00 | 30.86 | 18.54 | 31.00 | 43.66 | 44.23 | 44.78 | 45.32 | 45.85 |
| 36.00 | 30.53 | 19.08 | 32.00 | 44.06 | 44.61 | 45.15 | 45.68 | 46.20 |
| 36.00 | 30.19 | 19.61 | 33.00 | 44.42 | 44.96 | 45.48 | 46.00 | 46.51 |
| 36.00 | 29.85 | 20.13 | 34.00 | 44.74 | 45.26 | 45.78 | 46.28 | 46.78 |
| 36.00 | 29.49 | 20.65 | 35.00 | 45.02 | 45.53 | 46.03 | 46.53 | 47.01 |
| 36.00 | 29.12 | 21.16 | 36.00 | 45.26 | 45.76 | 46.25 | 46.73 | 47.21 |
| 36.00 | 28.75 | 21.67 | 37.00 | 45.46 | 45.95 | 46.43 | 46.90 | 47.36 |
| 36.00 | 28.37 | 22.16 | 38.00 | 45.63 | 46.10 | 46.57 | 47.02 | 47.48 |
| 36.00 | 27.98 | 22.66 | 39.00 | 45.75 | 46.21 | 46.66 | 47.11 | 47.55 |
| 36.00 | 27.58 | 23.14 | 40.00 | 45.82 | 46.27 | 46.72 | 47.15 | 47.58 |
| 36.00 | 27.17 | 23.62 | 41.00 | 45.86 | 46.29 | 46.73 | 47.15 | 47.57 |
| 36.00 | 26.75 | 24.09 | 42.00 | 45.85 | 46.27 | 46.69 | 47.11 | 47.51 |
| 36.00 | 26.33 | 24.55 | 43.00 | 45.79 | 46.21 | 46.62 | 47.02 | 47.41 |
| 36.00 | 25.90 | 25.01 | 44.00 | 45.69 | 46.10 | 46.49 | 46.89 | 47.27 |
| 36.00 | 25.46 | 25.46 | 45.00 | 45.55 | 45.94 | 46.33 | 46.71 | 47.09 |
| 36.00 | 25.01 | 25.90 | 46.00 | 45.36 | 45.74 | 46.12 | 46.49 | 45.85 |
| 36.00 | 24.55 | 26.33 | 47.00 | 45.13 | 45.50 | 45.86 | 46.23 | 46.58 |
| 36.00 | 24.09 | 26.75 | 48.00 | 44.85 | 45.21 | 45.56 | 45.92 | 46.26 |
| 36.00 | 23.62 | 27.17 | 49.00 | 44.53 | 44.88 | 45.22 | 45.56 | 45.90 |
| 36.00 | 23.14 | 27.58 | 50.00 | 44.16 | 44.50 | 44.83 | 45.16 | 45.49 |
| 37.00 | 32.04 | 18.50 | 30.00 | 45.27 | 45.86 | 46.43 | 47.00 | 47.55 |
| 37.00 | 31.72 | 19.06 | 31.00 | 45.74 | 46.31 | 46.87 | 47.42 | 47.96 |
| 37.00 | 31.38 | 19.61 | 32.00 | 46.16 | 46.72 | 47.27 | 47.81 | 48.33 |
| 37.00 | 31.03 | 20.15 | 33.00 | 46.55 | 47.09 | 47.63 | 48.15 | 48.57 |
| 37.00 | 30.67 | 20.69 | 34.00 | 46.90 | 47.43 | 47.95 | 48.46 | 48.97 |
| 37.00 | 30.31 | 21.22 | 35.00 | 47.20 | 47.72 | 48.23 | 48.73 | 49.22 |
| 37.00 | 29.93 | 21.75 | 36.00 | 47.47 | 47.97 | 48.47 | 48.96 | 49.44 |
| 37.00 | 29.55 | 22.27 | 37.00 | 47.69 | 48.18 | 48.67 | 49.15 | 49.61 |
| 37.00 | 29.16 | 22.78 | 38.00 | 47.87 | 48.35 | 48.82 | 49.29 | 49.74 |
| 37.00 | 28.75 | 23.28 | 39.00 | 48.01 | 48.47 | 48.93 | 49.39 | 49.83 |
| 37.00 | 28.34 | 23.78 | 40.00 | 48.09 | 48.55 | 49.00 | 49.44 | 49.87 |
| 37.00 | 27.92 | 24.27 | 41.00 | 48.14 | 48.58 | 49.02 | 49.45 | 49.87 |
| 37.00 | 27.50 | 24.76 | 42.00 | 48.14 | 48.57 | 48.99 | 49.41 | 49.82 |
| 37.00 | 27.06 | 25.23 | 43.00 | 48.09 | 48.51 | 48.92 | 49.33 | 49.73 |
| 37.00 | 26.62 | 25.70 | 44.00 | 47.99 | 48.40 | 48.80 | 49.20 | 49.59 |
| 37.00 | 26.16 | 26.16 | 45.00 | 47.85 | 48.24 | 48.63 | 49.02 | 49.40 |
| 37.00 | 25.70 | 26.62 | 46.00 | 47.66 | 48.04 | 48.42 | 48.80 | 49.17 |
| 37.00 | 25.23 | 27.06 | 47.00 | 47.42 | 47.79 | 48.16 | 48.52 | 48.88 |
| 37.00 | 24.76 | 27.50 | 48.00 | 47.13 | 47.49 | 47.85 | 48.21 | 48.56 |
| 37.00 | 24.27 | 27.92 | 49.00 | 46.79 | 47.15 | 47.50 | 47.84 | 48.13 |
| 37.00 | 23.78 | 28.34 | 50.00 | 46.41 | 46.75 | 47.09 | 47.43 | 47.76 |

Examination of the computer output indicates that the distance of the put is a function of release height. Theoretically this would indicate that, if an athlete could maintain the same release velocity, it would be to his advantage to put the shot from as high above the ground as possible. In practical terms, however, it means that the tall man with long arms has a natural advantage over his shorter opponent. This is confirmed by the physiques of world class shot putters.

The results also show that the release angle at which the maximum distance can be achieved varies directly with the magnitude of the release velocity (Table 4). This finding is not of great practical significance as there is only a four to five degree difference in the optimum angle between a release velocity of 26 feet per second (an inferior performance) and one of 46 feet per second (a performance exceeding present world standards). All other things being equal, the best angle of release for the shot is about 41 to 42 degrees with the horizontal.

The most important factor effecting the success of the shot put, however, is the magnitude of the release velocity. This is evident from both Table 4 and

Table 4

*Optimum Angle of Release of the Shot as a Function of Velocity and Height of Release*

| Resultant Release Velocity (Ft/Sec) | Height of Release (Ft) | | |
|---|---|---|---|
| | 6 | | 8 |
| 26 | 38 - 39*<br>(26.32)** | 37 - 38<br>(27.10) | 37<br>(27.87) |
| 30 | 40<br>(33.42) | 39<br>(34.24) | 39<br>(35.05) |
| 34 | 41<br>(41.47) | 40 - 41<br>(42.32) | 39 - 40<br>(43.16) |
| 38 | 42<br>(50.49) | 41<br>(51.37) | 40 - 41<br>(52.23) |
| 42 | 42<br>(60.48) | 42<br>(61.38) | 41<br>(62.27) |
| 46 | 43<br>(71.46) | 42<br>(72.37) | 42<br>(73.28) |

*Optimum release angle in degrees
**Number in brackets indicate the distance of the put in feet

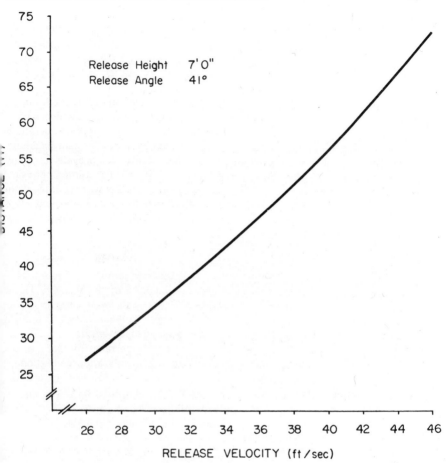

*Fig. 10. Shot Put Distance as a Function of the Magnitude of Release Velocity.*

Figure 10. The latter shows the distance as a function of release velocity when the height and angle of release are held constant. Therefore, for the best results, the stress should be upon increasing the speed of release of the shot even if it is at the expense of an optimum angle of projection.

This example of the computer simulation of a relatively simple system illustrates the steps involved in this type of research. Similar procedures could be extended equally well to investigate more complex systems.

**Summary**

Although computer simulation of human motion is of relatively recent origin, there has been a considerable upsurge in the number of models constructed since 1968. Researchers from the fields of aerospace engineering, rehabilitation medicine and sport have made major contributions in this area. Despite the apparent diversity of the biomechanical systems studies, similar steps have been followed in developing their simulation models. An appreciation of these procedures aids in understanding both the concept of simulation and the advantages and limitations of the technique. The recognition that simulation can never duplicate the real world exactly does not detract from the fact that it can provide important information concerning the mechanics of human performance. Computer simulation, however, is not a panacea. It will not furnish all the answers. It is a rather complex research technique which, in conjunction with other methods, may be used to advantage in studying the intricacies of human motion.

**Glossary**

*Analog Computer*—a computer which processes data of a continuous nature such as voltage changes.

*Boundary Values*—refer to the maximum and minimum values of a specific variable in a simulation model.

*Computer Graphics*—the pictorial display of digital computer results in the form of graphs, line diagrams or animated three dimensional drawings.

*Computer Simulation*—the process of studying the behaviour of systems utilizing a computerized mathematical model.

*Deterministic Model*—an analytical representation of a system or concept in which all the operating characteristics are exact relationships rather than probability functions. Therefore, there are unique outcomes for a given set of inputs.

*External Model*—a term used to refer to a deterministic computer simulation model concerned only with external forces acting upon a system. It does not include muscle and joint forces in the analysis.

*Hybrid Computer*—a computer which processes both analog and digital information.

*Initial Conditions*—the starting values of variable in a computer model at the beginning of a simulation.

*Input*—information fed into a computer program by the user.

*Internal Model*—a term referring to a deterministic biomechanical model which is concerned with the internal muscle and joint forces as well as with the forces external to the system.

*Linked System*—an idealized representation of the human body as a series of connected rigid segments.

*Mini Computer*—a small digital computer often used for the collection of data 'on-line' in a laboratory.

*Minimum Energy*—the principle which states that a normal person will automatically adjust his movements so that he expends a minimum of energy in performing a well-practiced skill like walking.

*Model*—usually refers to a mathematical representation of the components of a system and their interactions.

*Output*—results or information generated by a computer.

*Particle*—a body whose dimensions are negligible. When the human body is treated as a particle in a mechanical analysis, it is customarily represented by its mass centre.

*Program*—a series of instructions written in a computer language to accomplish one or more arithmetic or logical operations.

*Quasi-Rigid Body*—a body whose segments are capable of motion with respect to one another but which move together as a single unit for a designated time period.

*Rigid Body*—a body which undergoes negligible deformation. The individual segments of an athlete are often assumed rigid to facilitate mechanical analysis.

*Stochastic Model*—a representation of a system or concept in which some of the operating characteristics are subject to the laws of chance.

*System*—one or more distinct components which can interact to perform some function.

*Subroutine*—an independent set of computer instructions designed to perform some function in conjunction with the main computer program.

*Variable Name*—the designation given to a specific variable in a computer program.

**References**

BARTER, J.T. (1957). *Estimation of the mass of body segments.* WADC-TR-57-260. Wright-Patterson Air Force Base, Ohio.

BAUMANN, W. (1973). The influence of mechanical factors on speed at tobogganing. In S. Cerquiglini, A. Venerando & J. Wartenweiler (Eds.). *Biomechanics III,* Basel: Karger.

BECKETT, R. & CHANG, K. (1968). An evaluation of the kinematics of gait by minimum energy. *J. Biomechanics,* 1,147-159.

BRAUNE, W. & FISCHER, O. (1889). The centers of gravity in the human body. In W.M. Krogman & F.P. Johnston. *Human mechanics—four monographs abridged.* (1963) AMRL-TDR-63-123, Wright-Patterson Air Force Base, Ohio.

CHAFFIN, D.B. (1969). A computerized biomechanical model—development of and use in studying gross body actions. *J. Biomechanics, 2,* 429-441.

CHAFFIN, D.B. & BAKER, W.H. (1970). A biomechanical model for analysis of symmetric sagittal plane lifting. *AIIE Trans. Industrial Engineering Research and Development, 2,* 16-27.

CHEN, Y.R. & HUANG, B.K. (1970). Kinematics and computer simulation of human walking. Paper No. 70-663. American Society of Agricultural Engineers.

CHOW, C.K. & JACOBSON, D.H. (1972). Further studies of human locomotion: postural stability and control. *Math. Biosci., 15,* 93-108.

CHOW, C.K. & JACOBSON, D.H. (1971). Studies of human locomotion via optimal programming. *Math. Biosci., 10,* 239-310.

CLAUSER, C.E., MCCONVILLE, J.T. & YOUNG, J.W. (1969). *Weight, volume, and center of mass of segments of the human body.* AMRL-TR-69-70. Wright-Patterson Air Force Base, Ohio.

COCHRAN, A. & STOBBS, J. (1968). *The search for the perfect swing.* New York: Lippincott.

DEMPSTER, W.T. (1955). *Space requirements of the seated operator.* WADC-TR-55-159. Wright-Patterson Air Force Base, Ohio.

DILLMAN, C.J. (1971). A kinetic analysis of the recovery leg during sprint running. In J.M. Cooper (Ed.). *Selected Topics on Biomechanics.* Chicago: Athletic Institute.

DILLMAN, C.J. (1970). Muscular torque patterns of the leg during the recovery phase of sprint running. Unpublished doctoral dissertation, Pennsylvania State Univ.

FISCHER, O. (1906). Theoretical fundamentals for a mechanics of living bodies. In W.M. Krogman & F.P. Johnston (Eds.). *Human mechanics—four monographs abridged.* (1963). AMRL-TDR-63-123. Wright-Patterson Air Force Base, Ohio.

GALLENSTEIN, J. & HUSTON, R.L. (1973). Analysis of swimming motions. *Hum. Factors, 15,* 91-98.

GARRETT, G.E. & REED, W.S. (1971). Computer graphics: simulation techniques and energy analysis. In J.M. Cooper (Ed.). *Selected Topics on Biomechanics.* Chicago: Athletic Institute.

GARRETT, R., BOARDMAN, T. & GARRETT, G. (1973). Poor man's graphics—liberating a line. In S. Cerquiglini, A. Venerando & J. Wartenweiler (Eds.). *Biomechanics* III. Basel: Karger.

HANAVAN, E.P. (1964). *A mathematical model of the human body.* AMRL-TR-64-102. Wright-Patterson Air Force Base, Ohio.

HATZE, H. (1973). Optimization of human motions. In S. Cerquiglini, A. Venerando & J. Wartenweiler (Eds.). *Biomechanics III,* Basel: Karger.

JORGENSEN, L. (1970). On the dynamics of the swing of a golf club. *Am. J. Physics,* **38,** 644-651.

KULWICKI, P.V. & SCHLEI, E.J. (1962). *Weightless man: self-rotation techniques.* AMRL-TDR-62-129. Wright-Patterson Air Force Base, Ohio.

LINDSEY, G.R. (1963). An investigation of strategies in baseball. *Opns. Res.,* **11,** 477-501.

LINDSEY, G.R. (1961). The progress of the score during a baseball game. *Am. Stat. Assoc. J.,* **56,** 703-728.

LINDSEY, G.R. (1959). Statistical data useful for the operation of a baseball team. *Opns. Res.,* **7,** 197-207.

MILLER, D.I. (1973). Computer simulation of springboard diving. In S. Cerquiglini, A. Venerando & J. Wartenweiler (Eds.). *Biomechanics III.* Basel: Karger.

MILLER, D.I. (1971). A computer simulation model of the airborne phase of diving. In J.M. Cooper (Ed.). *Selected Topics on Biomechanics.* Chicago: Athletic Institute.

MILLER, D.I. (1970). A computer simulation model of the airborne phase of diving. Unpublished doctoral dissertation. Pennsylvania State Univ.

NUBAR, Y. & CONTINI, R. (1961). A minimal principle in biomechanics. *Bull. Math. Biophysics,* **23,** 377-391.

PEARSON, J.R., MCGINLEY, D.R. & BUTZEL, L.M. (1963). Dynamic analysis of the upper extremity: planar motions. *Hum. Factors,* **5,** 59-70.

PLAGENHOEF, S. (1971). *Patterns of Human Motion.* Englewood Cliffs, N.J.: Prentice-Hall.

QUIGLEY, B.M. & CHAFFIN, D.B. (1971). A computerized biomechanical model applied to the analysis of skiing. *Med. Sci. Sports,* **3,** 89-96.

RAMEY, M.R. (1973). The significance of angular momentum in long jumping. *Res. Quart.,* **44,** 35-42.

RAMEY, M.R. (1972). Effective use of force plates for long jump studies. *Res. Quart.,* **43,** 247-252.

RAMEY, M.R. (1970). Force relationships of the running long jump. *Med. Sci. Sports,* **2,** 146-151.

SEIREG, A. & BAZ, A. (1971). A mathematical model for swimming mechanics. In L. Lewillie & J.P. Clarys (Eds.). *Proceedings of the First International Symposium on Biomechanics in Swimming.* Brussels: Universite Libre de Bruxelles.

SMITH, P.G. & KANE, T.R. (1967). *The reorientation of a human being in free fall.* Technical Report No. 171, Div. of Eng. Mech., Stanford Univ.

WHITSETT, E.C. (1963). *Some dynamic response characteristics of weightless man.* AMRL-TDR-63-18. Wright-Patterson Air Force Base, Ohio.

WILLIAMS, D. (1967). The dynamics of the golf swing. *Quart. J. Mech. Appl. Math.,* **20,** 247-264.

**Bibliography**

BARTON, R.F. (1970). *A Primer on simulation and gaming.* Englewood Cliffs, New Jersey: Prentice-Hall.

BRICK, D.B. & CHASE, E.N. (1970) Interactive CRT display terminals. Part 1—The terminology and the market. *Modern Data,* **3,** 62-69 (May).

BRICK, D.B. & CHASE, E.N. (1970). Interactive CRT display terminals. Part 3—Graphic CRT terminals. *Modern Data,* **3,** 60-68 (July).

BRIGGS, W. G., HEXNER, J.T., MEYERS, R. & STEWART, M.G. (1960). A simulation of a baseball game. *Opns. Res.,* **8,** Supp. **2,** B-99.

CHASE, E.N. & BRICK, D.B. (1970). Interactive CRT display terminals. Part 2—Alphanumeric CRT terminals. *Modern Data.* **3,** 70-85 (June).

ESHKOL, N. et. al. (1970). *Notation of movement.* AD 703 936. Final Report, Department of Electrical Engineering, Univ. of Illinois.

FAIMAN, M. & NIEVERGELT, J. (Eds.) (1969). *Pertinent concepts in computer graphics.* Urbana, Illinois: University of Illinois Press.

FETTER, W.A. (1967). Computer graphics. *Design Quarterly,* **66/67,** 14-23.

FISCHER, B.O. (1967). Analysis of spinal stresses during lifting—a biomechanical model. Unpublished master's thesis, Univ. of Michigan.

GARRETT, G., REED, W.S., WIDULE, C. & GARRETT, R.E. (1971). Human motion: simulation and visualization. In J. Vredenbregt & J. Wartenweiler (Eds.). *Biomechanics II,* Basel: Karger.

GARRETT, R.E., WIDULE, C.J. & GARRETT, G.E. (1968). Computer—aided analysis of human motion. In *Kinesiology Review 1968,* Washington: AAHPER.

HUSTON, R.L. & PASSERELLO, C.E. (1971). On the dynamics of a human body model. *J. Biomech.,* **4,** 369-377.

KAHNE, S. & SALASIN, J. (1969). Computer simulation in athletic performance. In the *Proceedings of the Annual Meeting of the National College Physical Education Association—Men.* Chicago, Illinois, 25-29.

KANE, T.R., HEADRICK, M.R. & YATTEAU, J.D. (1972). Experimental investigation of an astronaut maneuvering scheme. *J. Biomech.,* **5,** 313-320.

KANE, T.R. & SCHER, M.P. (1970). Human self-rotation by means of limb movements. *J. Biomech.,* **3,** 39-49.

MARTIN, F.F. (1968). *Computer Modeling and Simulation.* New York: Wiley.

MCCRANK, J.M. & SEGER, D.R. (1964). *Torque free rotational dynamics of a variable configuration body (application to weightless man).* GAW/Mech 64-19. Wright-Patterson Air Force Base, Ohio.

MILNER, M. & QUANBURY, A.O. (1961). Programmed stimulation of skeletal muscle—some problems. In Vredenbregt, J. & Wartenweiler, J. (Eds.). *Biomechanics II.* Basel: Karger.

MILNER, M., BASMAJIAN, J.V. & QUANBURY, A.O. (1971). Multifactor analysis of walking by electromyography and computer. *Am. J. Phys. Med.,* **50,** 235-258.

MILNER, M., QUANBURY, A.O. & BASMAJIAN, J.V. (1970). Surface electrical stimulation of lower limb. *Arch. Phys. Med. Rehab.,* **51,** 540-546.

MILNER, M. & QUANBURY, A.O. (1970). Facets of control in human walking. *Nature,* **227,** 734-735.

MILNER, M., QUANBURY, A.O. & BASMAJIAN, J.V. (1969). Force, pain and electrode size in the electrical stimulation of leg muscles. *Nature,* **223,** 645.

MILSUM, J.H. (1968). Optimization aspects in biological control theory. In S.N. Levine (Ed.). *Advances in Biomedical Engineering and Medical Physics.* New York: Wiley.

MORAWSKI, J.M. (1973). Control systems approach to a ski turn analysis. *J. Biomech.,* **6,** 267-279.

PASSERELLO, C.E. & HUSTON, R.L. (1971). Human attitude control. *J. Biomech.,* **4,** 95-102.

PLAGENHOEF, S. (1968). Computer programs for obtaining kinetic data on human movement. *J. Biomech.,* **1,** 221-234.

PLAGENHOEF, S. (1963). Methods for obtaining kinetic data to analyze human motion. *Res. Quart.,* **37,** 103-112.

REED, W.S. & GARRETT, R.E. (1971). A three-dimensional human form and motion simulation. In *Kinesiology Review 1971.* Washington: AAHPER.

RIDDLE, C. & KANE, T.R. (1968). *Reorientation of the human body by means of arm motions.* Technical Report No. 182. Eiv. of Eng. Mech., Stanford Univ.

SECREST, D. & NIEVERGELT, J. (Eds.). (1968). *Emerging Concepts in Computer Graphics.* New York: W.A. Benjamin Inc.

SCHER, M.P. & KANE, T.R. (1969). *Alteration of the state of motion of a human being in free fall.* Technical Report No. 198, Div. of Eng. Mech., Stanford Univ.

SEIREG, A. & ARVIKAR, R.J. (1973). A mathematical model for evaluation of forces in lower extremities of the musculo-skeletal system. *J. Biomech.,* **6,** 313-326.

SMITH, P.G. & KANE, T.R. (1968). On the dynamics of the human body in free fall. *J. Appl. Mech.,* **35,** 167-168.

SNYDER, R.G., CHAFFIN, D.B. & SCHUTZ, K. (1971). *Link system of the human torso.* AMRL-TR-71-88. University of Michigan, Ann Arbor, Mich.

SUTHERLAND, I.E. (1970). Computer displays. *Sci. Amer.,* **222,** 56-81 (June).

TIEBER, J.A. & LINDEMUTH, R.W. (1965). *An analysis of the inertial properties and performance of the astronaut maneuvering system.* AMRL-TR-65-216. Wright-Patterson Air Force Base, Ohio.

TRUEMAN, R.E. (1959). A Monte Carlo approach to the analysis of baseball strategy. *Opns. Res.,* **7,** Supp. **2,** B-98.

YOUM, Y., HUANG, T.C., ZERNICKE, R.F. & ROBERTS, E.M. (1973). Mechanics of simulated kicking. In J.L. Bleustein (Ed.). *Mechanics and Sport.* New York: A.S.M.E.

# 4

# ELECTROMYOGRAPHY

# ELECTROMYOGRAPHY

by D.W. GRIEVE.

## Why record muscle activity?

As the techniques of photographic analysis, accelerometry, external force measurement and dynamic anthropometry develop, we become more certain about the calculations of the net forces and torques acting about chosen sections of the body during movement. An obvious development of the analysis is to extend our calculations so that we may attribute forces and torques to specific structures within the section. Bony structures may be under compression while ligaments, skin, muscles, fascia and tendons may be under tension. No system of external measurements will tell us what the state of affairs is within the body. We must resort to additional techniques if we are to apportion the contributions of various structures to the calculable net force or torque. The only techniques at our disposal are radiography, and possibly ultrasonics, which reveal the disposition of skeletal and other structures (e.g. indicating the regions of the articular surfaces which might be under compression), manometry, which may occasionally be used to determine the hydrostatic pressure within accessible cavities (e.g. abdominal cavity or an intervertebral disc) and electromyography. The latter is the most important and will be discussed at length.

Electromyography indicates when the muscles are electrically active. Although direct observation, palpation and mechanical sensing devices are of very limited scope, they were all that were available for assessing muscle action before the arrival of electromyography. Although crude, they at least had the merit of being concerned directly with the mechanical action of muscles. Electromyography is a very convenient and sensitive tool but it is an indirect indicator of muscle tension. Since biomechanics is largely concerned with mechanical actions, we must therefore consider the relationships that may be found or expected between the electrical and the mechanical activity.

There is another aspect of the electromyogram which is also of interest. Muscles are effector organs of the nervous system. The efferent signals transmitted by the nervous system are too weak to be detected directly during normal voluntary activity but the electromyogram may be regarded as an index of efferent alpha-motoneurone activity, and closely related to it in time. For those who are concerned with the coordination of body action, it is therefore a matter of interest as to how accurate and valid a description of the EMG may be obtained, not for predictive purposes mentioned above, but simply as an accessible index of the efferent nervous activity.


## The Electromyogram

An electromyogram is a record of the fluctuations of potential that occur between two conducting (metal) surfaces that are either placed on the surface of the body or within it, due to the electrical activity of the muscles. Distinguishable signals may be as small as $10\mu V$ and the strongest signals rarely exceed 5mV. The power at input is less than $10^{-12}$ watt, so that both voltage and power amplification is necessary to obtain a recording. An electromyogram at input contains frequency components from a few Hz up to several kHz Nightingale (1957), Chaffin (1969), Sato et al. (1965) (see Fig. 1) and the frequency content is affected by physiological condition e.g. fatigue, changes of muscle temperature and disease. Electromyographs differ widely in their frequency response and, in spite of this, many reports appear without stating what the frequency characteristics of the machine are. Secondly, the visual appearance of an electromyogram is greatly affected by the speed at which the recorder operates, the gain of the recorder and the nature of the recording medium. The investment in diverse instruments is so great that standardisation is currently impracticable. The gradual introduction of computers into bio-mechanics laboratories for the recording and processing of muscle signals in digital form may eventually lessen the influence of the chart type electro-myogram, but at present our way of regarding the record and communicating to each other about them are strongly linked to the visual appearance. These technical aspects of recording should therefore be considered when a description of the electromyogram is made or read.


## Electromyographic equipment

A modern electromyograph usually consists of a pre-amplifier, a main amplifier and a selection of recording devices. Modular equipment is common, which is capable of handling non-electromyographic signals also, from strain gauge or displacement transducers for example, simply by changing the pre-amplifier. In these cases the main amplifiers are direct-coupled amplifiers with balance and gain controls and selection of the high-frequency attenuation which in any case is steep above about 10kHz. Only the pre-amplifier is specifically designed for handling signals from the body-tissues. It is desirable to

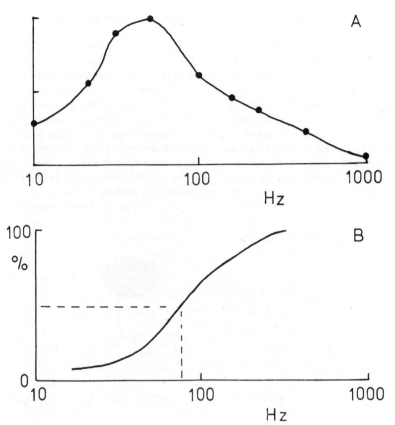

*Fig. 1. Frequency analysis of surface electromyograms of limb musculature. A: from Chaffin (1969). B: in cumulative form, from Sato et al. (1965).*

draw as little current from the body as possible. (The input impedance is usually in the range 2-10 Megohms) The signals usually exist in the presence of much greater common-mode signals. The pre-amplifier is for this reason a balanced differential amplifier with a high common-made rejection of approximately 100,000:1. The signal spectrum ranges from 20Hz–2000Hz approximately, which can be be suitably handled by a capacity-coupled pre-amplifier. The low frequency attenuation is selectable. Noise levels referred to input should not exceed 10$\mu$VR.M.S. and maybe as low as 2$\mu$VR.M.S. over the range of signal frequencies. Readers who are contemplating electromyography should consult and compare the specifications in the sales literature of the manufacturers together with a text of medical electronics. One feature that is not usually mentioned is the stability of the instrument especially as regards gain, and this is relevant if quantitative work is envisaged.

A choice of outputs of the main amplifier is usually provided. An output of low impedance (tens of ohms) is suitable for driving optical galvanometers whilst an output of high impedance e.g. 2 kilohms, is suitable for driving cathode ray oscillographs and digitisers. Optical galvanometers may be obtained which respond to frequencies as high as 3kHz, i.e. to the complete spectrum of the electromyogram as does the cathode ray oscilloscope. Pen writing oscillographs, on the other hand, never respond to the full frequency range and may be limited to 100 Hz. Another type of galvanometer recorder writes with a jet of ink and, because of the low inertia mass of the device, can respond to frequencies as high as 400Hz. Assuming that the speed of the chart is sufficient for the details of the trace to be resolved, the appearances of the records at these frequency limits are quite different, as is shown in Fig. 2. It is very unusual for EMG records made for purposes of studying movements to use chart speeds sufficient to resolve the fine detail. For example, resolution of a 1kHz signal requires a chart speed of

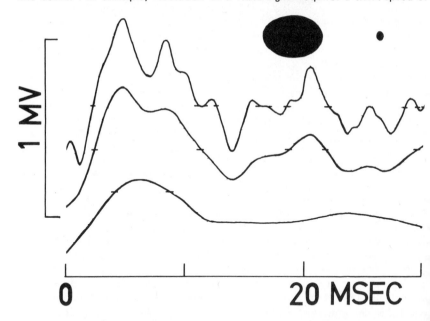

Fig. 2. Bipolar surface electromyograms (5 cm vertical spacing, biceps brachii), drawn from digital data. Upper trace: all frequencies present from data sampled at 10kHz. Frequency contents similar to that recorded by ink-jet recorder (middletrace) and by EEG pen recorder (Lower trace) obtained by recursive digital filtering of original signal. The closed ellipses show the approximate extremes of recorder spots (5mV/cm, 10cm/sec on left, 0.1mV/cm & 100cm/sec on right) that are used by various investigators without standardisation.

1m/sec. if the trace is 0.5mm. thick. If 6 channels (or more) are recorded simultaneously (which limits the width available for each), and chart speeds are limited for practical reasons of economy or simply to permit features of the whole movement to be seen at a glance, it is probably of very little importance whether the amplifier is linear to better than 5% of full scale deflection, whether the recorder is responding to more than a few hundred Hz or whether the input impedance is low or not. The eye would not appreciate the effects of improved linearity or of a higher frequency response. Good in-phase rejection, on the other hand, is essential regardless of other qualities; the ubiquitous 'mains hum' is the bane of electromyographers.

It is increasingly the practice to quantify the EMG in some way e.g. integrate, or count spikes. It is a wise precaution to obtain a visual record at the same time as a check that the signals are normal in appearance and free from artifact. The quantification places a much higher premium upon such factors as stability and linearity. The capacity for simultaneous quantification of several channels on-line with hard-wired devices, apart from its expense, may prove very restrictive. As far as the quantification of phasic electromyographic signals is concerned, there is no general agreement at present as to the most suitable technique (or even whether a quantitative result is more useful than a visual judgment). In the present state of the art it is advisable for laboratories to choose general purpose rather than specialised electromyographic equipment. Investment in custom-built multi-channel machines which are only capable of performing one type of quantification is not justified at present.

The flexible approach at modest cost is to use an F.M. tape-recorder and process the data either by multiple replays through selected single channels of custom-built analogue analysers. An alternative is to digitise the information and use a small general purpose computer to process the data. A digitised record gives enormous flexibility to the processing of EMG data. If sufficient storage capacity exists then the same signals can be processed in many alternative ways. The cost of amplifying, digitising, processing and storing multichannel EMG data can be very high indeed. If the raw data is stored, approximately 4000 3-decade numbers are needed for every second of recording on a single channel if all possibilities of future processing are to be preserved. Multichannel-work, e.g. 12 channels for as little as 20 seconds may require hours of computing in the central processor unit (CPU time) even on a large machine such as the IBM 360 when several alternative quantifications are attempted. A smaller and slower machine may only give flexibility in principle and seemingly modest projects assume frightening proportions. Time for thought about the electromyograms may easily be replaced by time for data handling and for devising ingenuous software to do so (Black, 1971). Final results draw in Indian ink on a Calcomp plotter may be very beautiful but the laboratory staff pay heavily for it in time and machine involvement.

The sensible middle course of on-line processing and data reduction before storage will probably emerge at some stage but the transition from simply looking at traces to examining quantitative descriptions has only just started. Much wider agreement about the significance of a quantitative result, i.e. its repeatability, applicability and predictive value, is needed before standardised machines are accepted. The modest number of laboratories with access to the large digital machines can make a useful contribution here, not particularly by making kinesiological discoveries but by exploring the relative merits of simple analogue or hybrid EMG analyses which can be simulated in the first instance by the large general purpose machine. The sooner this phase in the development of electromyographic kinesiology is over the better as far as standardisation and effective communication are concerned.

## Choice of recording electrodes

The electrodes may be as minute as the exposed ends of fine wires embedded in the tip of an hypodermic needle which is pushed through the skin into the muscle of interest. The needle electrode is the most common type in use for clinical diagnostic purposes but is utterly unsuited for studies of movement and will therefore be dismissed. At the other extreme, the electrodes may be approximately 1 cm. diameter silver-silver chloride discs or cups placed on the skin surface, separated from it only by a layer of chloride-containing jelly. (Chloride ions are common to the electrodes, the jelly and the body tissues.) These surface electrodes (of which there are many varieties) are popular in biomechanical work, as also are wire electrodes, which take the form of a pair of twisted Karma-alloy wires, nylon insulated except for the region near their tips. The wire electrodes are introduced into a muscle by means of a hypodermic needle, which is then withdrawn, leaving the wires *in situ* like two fine fish hooks.

There is no doubt about the superiority of wire electrodes for obtaining recordings from deeply placed muscles, *if they can be located.* As to other relative advantages of surface and wire electrodes, it is very instructive to compare Basmajian (1968) and Jonsson (1968) on the subject. Basmajian, conceding the ease with which surface electrodes may be applied, claims that they are only suitable for investigating the interplay between widely separated muscle groups in preliminary studies.

Since kinesiological studies of the interplay of widely separated muscle groups have hardly scratched the surface of the problems, we should not perhaps be too discouraged by this. It is an assertion that must have been based upon direct experience because our limited knowledge of the factors determining the surface potential do not permit theoretical predictions to be made. The action potentials in mammalian muscle according to Pattle (1971) cause potential changes at a distance as if they were miniature electric dipoles. The field of a

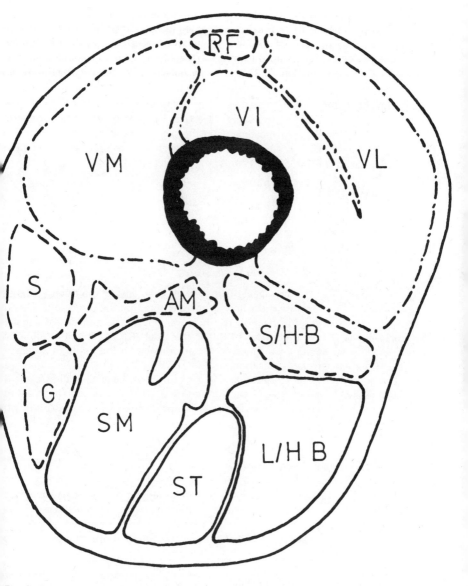

Fig. 3. Transverse section of thigh. VM, VI, VL & RF refer to quadriceps group. SM, ST & L/H-B refer to hamstrings. S/H-B, AM, S & G refer to short head of biceps, adductor magnus, sartorius and gracilis muscles. Section used for speculation as to relative importance of various muscles as contribution to surface electromyograms, featured in Fig. 4.

dipole diminishes as the inverse square of the distance in the range that concerns surface recording. If one considers a cross section of a thigh for example (Fig. 3) and gives each element of area in each muscle a weighting proportional to the inverse square of the distance from a surface site, a 'view' of the musculature is obtained as shown in Fig. 4. This is a very naive approach, easy to criticise but

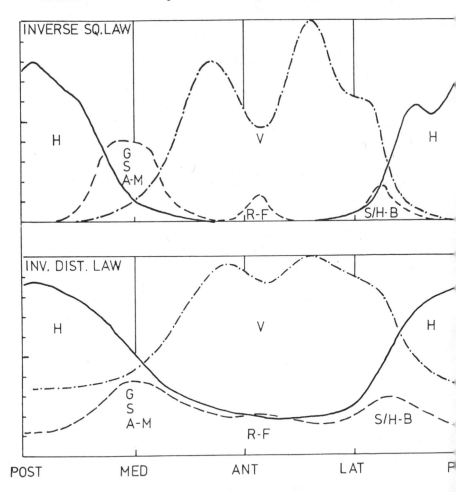

Fig. 4. Possible 'views' of the muscles as seen from electrode sites around the limb circumference at the level of section given in Fig. 3. The upper set assumes that activity in an element of muscle section exerts an effect at the surface proportional to the inverse square of the distance from it. An inverse distance law is assumed for the lower set which, if true, leads to lower selectivity of the surface electromyogram.

difficult to improve upon, except to consider that the muscles in fact extend on either side of the section. If dipoles (coaxial) with muscles of double infinite extent) are equally likely to occur in all regions of a muscle, an alternative weighting of the section elements is suggested of inverse distance. The 'view' obtained from points on the skin surface is then given by Fig. 4. Although very little hard evidence can be produced to support either model, practical experience suggests that the first model approximates to the 'view' obtained from surface electromyography and bears out Basmajian's remarks. It is possible to choose electrode sites to investigate the interplay of the hamstring group and the vasti for example. A confused picture is obtained from the medial aspect of the thigh at the level of the section and it is not possible to say anything about the function of, say, the short head of biceps by means of surface electromyography. A model based upon the inverse square weighting of muscle sections in the calf seems to account more satisfactorily for the 'cross talk' observed between the anterior tibial musculature and the calf muscles during simultaneous recordings than does the 'inverse distance' model, but much more work is required to produce a model of general validity for the limbs.

The placement of surface electrodes is both an art and a science. Surface electrodes do not respond solely to the muscles that underlie them, i.e. it is not sufficient to place electrodes where the muscle's bulge can be seen. Suppose that muscles A and B are in close relation to each other while it is desired to record signals from A alone. This may be impossible with surface electrodes although, if enough is known about the actions A and B, it is sometimes possible to devise exercises for the subject which call for activity in A and B separately. If so, electrode positions may then be chosen by trial and error which show a marked sensitivity to A and little to B. Not only does this require a familiarity with muscle action such as a physiotherapist would possess, but it also begs the question if the manner of use of the muscle is in dispute, at least at a quantitative level. It would be very much more satisfactory if we could 'see' the muscles in the way that the electrodes 'see' them and base our choice of sites upon this model. A theoretical approach is not likely to be very profitable at present since our knowledge of the field patterns due to populations of muscle fibres under normal conditions of excitation is at present too rudimentary to provide this insight. There is scope for a direct empirical approach by recording from many surface sites and wire-electrode sites simultaneously with a view to determining the extent to which valid conclusions about individual muscles can be drawn from surface recording.

Basmajian (1968) further condemns the use of surface electrodes for the study of fine movement, for detecting the presence or absence of activity and in all circumstances where 'scientific precision is required'. Jonsson (1968) is more specific as regards the precision to be expected from wire electrodes. In experiments with brachioradialis, in which the strength of contraction was carefully standardised, the mean voltage recorded was found to be a function of both the length of the exposed tips and the interelectrode distance. The latter factor alone gave rise to 20% variations in the mean voltage. Jonsson published radiographs of the wire electrodes *in situ* before and after a few muscle contractions and it is clear that the geometry of the wires is unstable. Anyone who has experimented with excised living muscle knows how easily damaged are the muscle fibres and how the release of potassium from injured cells affects neighbouring cells. It seems possible that at least some of the fibres close to the electrode tips are dead during an intramuscular recording and that the membrane potentials and action potentials in the immediate vicinity are abnormal.

Basmajian claims that the pick-up area of wire electrodes having 1mm tips is confined either to the whole muscle or to the fascicle containing them because the layer of fibrous connective tissue acts as insulation. Examination of the fibrous septa in and between muscles suggest otherwise. It seems highly unlikely that the fluid-filled interstices of the septa present any greater barrier to the passage of ionic currents than do the intracellular spaces elsewhere. The pick-up area is of course much more limited than that of surface electrodes. This could be a valuable feature when a small number of motor units are to be studied, but there does not appear to be firm evidence that the information from wire electrodes is any more representative of the activity of a muscle (a superficial one, at least), than that from surface electrodes.

There may also be some doubt about the anatomical locations of the wire tips which has been resolved in some experiments by injecting carbon dioxide into the region so that a radiographic outline of the local fascial planes is obtained. Jonsson sounds a further word of caution that a high incidence of wire fracture (25%) may be expected in vigorous movements when 25 micra wires are used and an appreciable incidence when the thicker 50 micra wires are used. From a quantitative standpoint, the fracture may be undetected during visual examination of the recording yet still produce a change in the mean recorded voltages. Shorting of the wires is a further complication that may occur. Whether experiments are done by the medically qualified or not, the ethics of leaving wire fragments in the body and resorting to radiographs to locate the electrode sites for non-clinical purposes seems questionable, to say the least. The reader would doubtless refer to the published work before embarking on an electromyographic project but it may be that surface electrodes are not only safer, easier to use and more acceptable to the subject, but, for superficial muscles at least, provide a degree of quantative repeatability that compares favourably with wire electrodes.


## Is a Relationship to be expected between Mechanical or Metabolic Parameters and the Electromyogram?

It would be very valuable if there were some way in which the active tension in a muscle, or its rate of work, rate of oxygen consumption or some other interesting physiological parameter, could be predicted from the electromyogram. Success in predicting tension from electromyograms under isometric conditions, e.g. Lippold (1952), has led to a general conviction that the mechanical tension should be predictable in the general case, providing that the EMG waveform can be suitably processed. To quote from Sorbie & Zalter (1964) concerning some locomotor studies, "although no exact quantitative correlation between muscle tension and electrical activity is assumed, the amplitude of electrical activity displayed by a muscle can be considered to reflect the level of muscle tension". The following pages are devoted to the discussion of some properties of a motor-unit that are relevant to its use in dynamic conditions. It will be seen that the electromyogram may have predictive value for the tension in a muscle, provided not only that the measure used is a useful index of the active state of the population of muscle fibres but also that the mechanical conditions under which the muscle is operating are described. *Unless both factors are taken into account the interpretation is likely to be ambiguous or indeterminate.* Predictions of tension from electromyograms in the general case lie in the future, and the prediction of oxygen consumption does also. If methods of prediction could be established however, most important consequences would follow for linking biomechanical studies with physiological studies.

Much time has elapsed since the isometric relationships were discovered and, although other relationships have been reported in special circumstances, it is still true to say that no general rules of prediction have been found. Since it is the almost universal practice to at least infer an increase of tension when an increase in the amplitude of the electromyogram occurs, it is instructive to consider the nature of the relationship further.

The unit event within a muscle in the near-synchronous firing of the muscle fibres in a motor unit due to the arrival of an impulse in their common motor nerve fibre. If tension can be predicted from the electrical activity of one such unit then the EMG of the whole muscle might be expected to have predictive value. At the site of a recording electrode, the potential change due to the action potentials in all these muscle fibres will have a particular temporal form. The exact form will depend upon many factors, i.e. the electrode position, the degree of synchrony within the motor unit, the geometry of the fibres in relation to the neuromuscular junctions and the chemical composition of the body fluids in the muscle and the geometry of the surrounding tissues. The potential changes *in vivo* are virtually complete before they can be repeated i.e. their time course is of the order of 2-5 millisecond, while repetition rates are unlikely to exceed 50 per second. Repetitions do not occur regularly, although the regularity increases i.e. variance of time between impulses decreases, as the mean repetition rate rises.

Activity in another motor unit will give rise to its particular pattern of potential change at the electrode. The lack of quantitative information about the patterns of firing rates in a population of motor units is one of the factors which prevents realistic models of electromyograms to be developed. Although the unit contributions to a recorded electromyogram are discreet all-or-nothing events which sum algebraically, the mechanical results of them are not. That is to say, the mechanical state does not necessarily return to the resting level before the arrival of a further nerve impulse. The mechanical consequences of electrical activity in the motor units cannot therefore be represented as the algebraic sum of unit mechanical events, one for each action potential.

Although a purist would further query whether the mechanical effects of activity in the fibres of a motor unit could be considered as the sum of synchronous mechanical effects in the separate fibres, it seems likely to be close to the truth. The reasons for this are that the time taken to initiate activation after arrival of the nerve impulse is short compared with the duration of the mechanical effects which follow, and all the fibres in one unit are of similar type, histologically at least. The fibres also occupy a localised region within the whole muscle so that the lengths of each are similar and the lengths of tendon attached to each are also similar.

Consider Fig. 5. The arrival of an action potential in the motor nerve gives

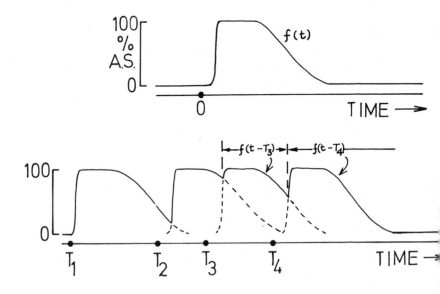

Fig. 5. A. Time course f(t) of active state (schematic) following arrival of single impulse at time zero. B. Time course of active state as result of a train of nerve impulses arriving at times T1, T2 etc.

rise to an active state in the motor unit. This is defined as the ability of the contractile part of the motor unit to develop tension or to shorten, if the mechanical conditions permit it. It does not follow that the unit will do either of these things at the instant that the ability, i.e. the active state, is established. The reason may be that external mechanical conditions prevent shortening or that structures in series with the unit are not sufficiently stiff at that instant for tension to be transmitted. It is most unusual for tension to develop in the contractile element without a change of length also. The change of length may be a shortening but it is just as common for stretching to be in progress when activation occurs, the purpose of the activation being to control or reverse the stretching.

The contractile element that has been mentioned several times already is an abstraction in the sense that it does not possess an anatomical identity. It is that part of the motor unit between the attachments which is responsible for the development of tension at the expense of metabolic energy. The regions of the actomyosin arrays, in particular where the actin and myosin filaments overlap, contain the contractile element. However, parts of the array may act as passive structures which transmit the tension but play no part in its development. The sum of the non-active structures in series with the active contractile element is referred to as the series elastic element and also has no clear anatomical identity. The elasticity, like that of most biological material, is non-Hookian, i.e. non-linear. Stiffness increases with the degree of stretch. In addition to the series elastic element, there are passive structures in the muscle, such as the sarcolemmal sheaths of the muscle fibres and the connective tissue bindings around the fibre bundles (endo- and perimysium) which will develop tension passively when stretched, independently of the tension in the contractile and series elastic elements. For this reason, these structures are collectively represented by and referred to as the parallel elastic element. The parallel elastic element is responsible for all the tension within a resting muscle under static conditions, and for much of the tension in a fully active muscle when it is greatly stretched. Because fluid movements may occur through restricted spaces within the muscle during movement, viscoelastic elements may also have a place in exact models of muscle. Viscoelastic behaviour may also be exhibited by the collagen in the series and parallel elastic elements although it can probably be disregarded to a first approximation under physiological conditions.

It is now appropriate to consider what happens to the tension in a motor unit on receipt of a nerve impulse. The active state develops rapidly in all regions when the muscle action potentials reach them. The conduction of the muscle action potential occurs at rates of up to 20 metres per second. Because distances of 100 mm or less from the end plate are usually involved, all regions of the muscle fibres begin their activity cycle within about 5 msec. Buchtal, Guld & Rosenfalck (1957) found temporal dispersions of action potentials of this order within a motor unit. At any particular site along a muscle fibre, the active state develops fully within a few milliseconds. The combined delays of conduction and the onset of active state probably entail a delay of the order of 5-10 msec from the arrival of a nerve impulse to the full establishment of active state in every part of the contractile apparatus. The single period of active state, which develops fully in a few milliseconds, persists at an approximately maximum level for tens of milliseconds. The durations of the active states in human motor units have not been studied as extensively as they have in other mammals and in amphibia (Close, 1972). It is not certain whether a true plateau of active state is reached in mammalian fibres, as distinct from the cold amphibian muscle fibres which have been studied extensively. Judging from Buchtal and Schmalbruch's (1970a) measurements of contraction times almost full active state may persist for periods of 20 millisecond when the motor units are of the fast (white) type and 60 millisecond or longer in the case of slow (red) units. On histological evidence, both slow and fast types are to be found in most, if not all, human skeletal muscle, but we do not know whether there is a continuum of physiological properties from very fast to very slow to be found, or whether there are functionally distinct groups as regards the speed of contraction and the duration of active state.

Let us suppose that the intensity of active state at time t is a function $f(t - T_1)$ of the time from receipt at $T_1$ of a solitary nerve impulse. During a train of nerve impulses at time T1, T2, T3 etc, the active state at any instant is equal to the maximum value of $f(t - T1)$, $f(t - T2)$, $f(t - T3)$ etc.

When the motor unit receives a second nerve impulse, the active state curve follows a time course similar to that due to the first, as soon as the intensity in the second time course exceeds that which has persisted from the first activation. The active state curves are not additive (at least to a first approximation—although this statement may need revision when more is known about mammalian muscle) and we may assign an intensity corresponding to the last nerve impulse received providing that it exceeds that corresponding to the previous impulse. It is easier to express this visually than put it into words because there is no terminology that can be borrowed from a similar phenomenon in other fields. In Fig. 5A a single active state has been depicted. The active state curve due to a succession of nerve impulses is shown in 5B. The active state persists at full intensity (ignoring the influence of fatigue) if nerve impulses arrive sufficiently frequently. This would happen at a frequency of about 50 impulses per second in fast fibres and about 15 per second in slow fibres. There is little quantitative information about the rates of firing of motor nerves in humans although Bigland & Lippold (1954a) found rates up to but not exceeding 50 per second. An individual unit increases its rate of firing rapidly with the tension in the whole muscle once its threshold of onset if reached. With further increases of tension, the firing rate reaches a plateau and then increases more rapidly at very high tensions. This behaviour was found in voluntary contractions of abductor digit minimi and it is not known whether this is a general feature of other muscles or not. It is a general feature for the number of turning points in an electromyogram (both wire and surface) to increase rapidly with the tension in a muscle (see Fig. 17) until a plateau is reached. Further increase may occur as maximum tensions are approached. Although this is reminiscent of Bigland & Lippold's observations, we do not know how the interference pattern of the electromyogram is related to the patterns of the individual motor units.

It is worth remembering that the performance of a body movement may only require the use of a particular muscle group for a few tenths of a second. Less than ten impulses in a particular motor unit may be involved and the patterns of firing during voluntary movement, as distinct from steady contractions, have not been described. The patterning of these short bursts of impulses, providing that the time interval between impulses is greater than the plateau of the active state, can produce many subtle variations on the resultant fluctuation of active state. These variations, as well as the distribution of them amongst the motor units, presumably are the basis of the differences in performance between skilled and clumsy movement. The recognition of the quality of a movement comes from its mechanical result, not from the accompanying electromyograms and, rather than digress further, it is appropriate to return to the main consideration of whether the electromyogram provides a predictive tool for the estimation of the mechanical consequences. Clearly, if it did so, it would greatly strengthen the case for assessing the electromyogram in a quantitative manner.

The three-component model of a motor unit may be represented diagrammatically as shown in Fig. 6. The total length of the muscle, $L_p$, is also the length of the parallel elastic element. This equals the combined length of the contractile element, $L_C$, and the series elastic element, $L_S$. The total tension transmitted by the muscle is the sum of the tension, $T_2$, in the parallel elastic element, and the tension, $T_1$, in the contractile and series elastic elements.

Two properties of the model motor unit are unaffected by the activity. These, illustrated in Fig. 6A and B, are the tension-length characteristics of the series and parallel elastic elements. Two further properties (see C & D) are those of the active contractile element. Diagram C depicts the tension-length characteristic and D shows the tension-velocity characteristic, (commonly referred to as the force-velocity curve). The tension $T_0$, which appears on diagrams A and B (Fig. 6) represents the maximum possible tension that the contractile element can exert under isometric conditions. At any instant, when the active state is a fraction of the maximum possible intensity, the tension $T_1$ is given by the product:

$$T_1 = \alpha \beta \gamma \, T_0$$

where $\alpha$ = intensity of active state/maximum intensity $T_0$

$\gamma$ = tension at velocity $L_C$/isometric tension at the same length and same intensity of active state

$\beta$ = (isometric tension at length $L_C$)/$T_0$

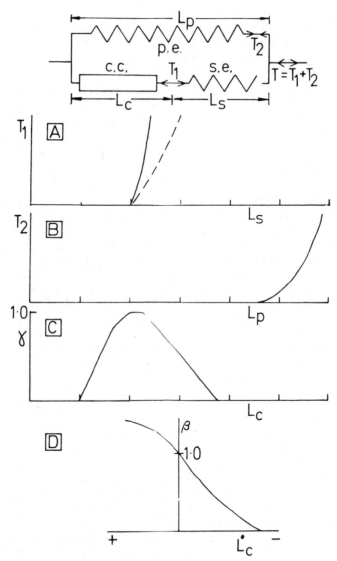

*Fig. 6. Schematic diagrams of 3-component model of a muscle. The non-linear tension-extension characteristics of the series and parallel elastic elements are shown in A & B respectively. The isometric tension in the fully active (α = 1) contractile element is length dependent and shown as a fraction, γ of the maximum isometric tension in C. In addition, the tension of the contractile element is velocity dependent and is shown as a fraction β of the isometric tension (at any length) in D.*

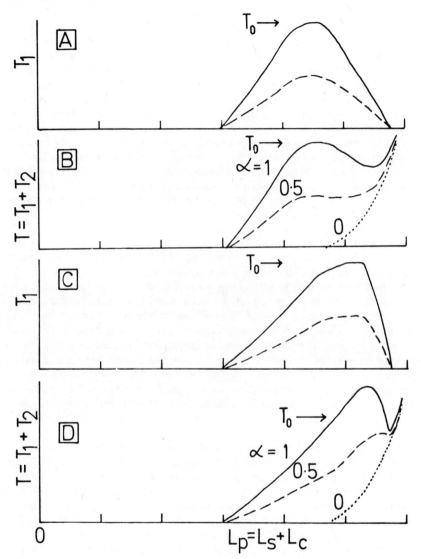

Fig. 7. The isometric tension-length curve of the whole muscle is described in Fig. 6. The 'active-tension'-length curve in A is shown dashed for a state of partial activation α = 0.5. Note the shift in the form of the curve in C which corresponds to the dashed series elastic characteristic of fig. 6A. B & D (corresponding to A & C respectively) show the isometric tension in the whole muscle, which includes the effect of parallel elasticity for partially and fully active muscle (α = 0, 0.5 and 1.0 respectively).

Consider first the tension produced under isometric conditions (which is a rare physiological state). The system is static from a mechanical point of view so that $\gamma = 1$. At a given level, $\alpha$, of active state, tension $T_1$ may be expressed as a function of the total length of the muscle $(L_s + L_c)$ by combining charts A and C of Fig. 6. The result is shown in A of Fig. 7 for various intensities of active state. If the effect of the parallel elastic element is added, chart B is obtained. In practice, only $\alpha = 1$ (full tetanic tension), or $\alpha = 0$ (rest) can be achieved under steady isometric conditions. Other values of $\alpha$ may exist but are not stable. Intermediate intensities fluctuate rapidly because they only arise as the result of trains of nerve impulse arriving at sub-tetanic rates and isometric conditions in the motor unit are only achieved for brief instants, twice per nerve impulse.

In the present context, the point to be made is that the active state which is obviously related to and conceivably predictable from the electromyogram, is only one determinant of the tension. Unless the mechanical conditions are also known, no measure of the electromyogram can predict the tension.

The preceding model assumes that the muscle fibre (or the contractile component) is homogeneous during activity which is certainly true if it is tetanically active but is not necessarily the case in a twitch or in sub-tetanic states. Mammalian muscle is very much faster in its action than the ubiquitous cold frog muscles and it may prove necessary to consider fibres which are beginning to relax in one region while activity is still fully maintained at another.

Consider a motor unit whose fibres possess endplates at their centres. Fig. 8 illustrates in schematic form how the intensity of active state varies with both time and distance along the fibre measured from the end plate upon receipt of a nerve impulse. The end silhouette on the right represents the time course of active state at any point along a fibre. Because of the finite conduction velocity, this temporal change occurs at the end plate region first and in other places later. By means of Fig. 8 it is possible to visualise the course of activation throughout the fibres and to appreciate the interaction of conduction velocity, length of fibre and time course of active state.

Consider a fibre of length A $A^1$ as depicted. The profiles which have been drawn around the diagram represent the active state intensity along the fibre at various times apart. As shown, it can be seen that the fibre is never fully activated along its length during a twitch. For the particular combination of conduction velocity and active state duration, it can be seen that a fibre of length B $B^1$ would be fully activated for part of the twitch. In Fig. 8 a doubling of the conduction velocity is equivalent to considering fibre B $B^1$ instead of A $A^1$. In a similar way, a reduction of the active state duration to one half, in the absence of any other change, is equivalent to replacing a fibre of length B $B^1$ by one of length A $A^1$. Although there is no quantitative treatment given here because little is known of the particular combinations of quantities in man, it is likely that single twitches in at least some muscles in man occur without full activation throughout the length of a fibre. One implication of this is that the

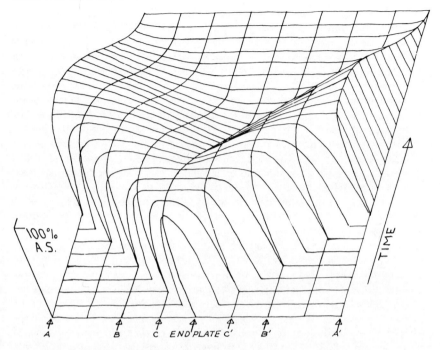

*Fig. 8. The change of intensity of active state in a muscle fibre after its initiation at a centrally-placed end-plate. Distant regions of the fibre undergo the same temporal changes of active state as at the end plate but at a later time because of the conduction delay. Comparison of fibres $BB^1$ or $CC^1$ with $AA^1$ is equivalent to doubling or trebling the conduction velocity. The possibility of variations of active state with distance from the end plate complicates the time course of the effective active state in the model of Fig. 6 and the effective series-elasticity becomes time dependent.*

effective stiffness of the 'series elastic element' could be time dependent (unlike the state of affairs in which the motor unit is tetanically active). As was seen in the earlier discussion of tension-length curves, the effect of a decrease in stiffness of the series-elastic element is to shift the kurtosis of the tension-length curve towards the right. It is interesting in this connection that Rack & Westbury (1969) found that the sarcomere spacing in cats' soleus for development of twitch tension was at about 2.9, much more than Gordon *et al.* (1966) found in amphibian muscle fibres.

Another relevant aspect of the electromyogram which we may consider graphically is the time separation between the electrical activity and the mechanical effect. Let us suppose that at time zero the intensity of active state changes rapidly from $\alpha = 0$ to $\alpha = 1.0$. For present purposes we shall consider this as an instantaneous change. Three cases will be considered in which the whole motor unit is (a) being stretched, (b) isometric and (c) shortening at steady rates respectively. To simplify matters, it will be assumed that the total change of length is insufficient to affect $\beta$. Therefore in these examples $\alpha = \beta = 1.0$ after time zero. A further simplification is made that the parallel elastic element remains slack. It is not difficult to find an 'actual' activity involving maximal effort which operates under these conditions. Tension $T_1$ depends on the rate of movement $L_c$ of the contractile element as shown in A of Fig. 9. The difference between the rate of movement, $\dot{L}p$, of the whole unit (see B) and $Lc$, of the contractile element, is the rate of change of length, $\dot{L}s$, of the series elastic element, shown in (c). The stiffness and rate of stretch of the series elastic element is expressed as a function of tension in [D]. The product of stiffness and rate of stretch is the rate of change of tension as shown in [E]. Its reciprocal in [F] is the time taken for unit change of tension, expressed as a function of tension. The definite integral of function [F] between the limits of zero tension and tension T1 is the time taken for the tension to rise to T1.

The tension in case 1, i.e. during an eccentric contraction rises at a much higher rate than in case 3, i.e. during concentric contraction, although the active state of the motor unit is the same in both cases. At present we do not know whether the electromyogram from a whole muscle will predict the tension or not in the general case, even if the mechanical conditions are defined. Even with the simplifying assumptions that have been introduced, it is obvious that the changes of tension in a muscle following identical bursts of electromyographic activity differ in both their magnitude and their time course depending upon the mechanical conditions. There is therefore no possibility of predicting tension from the electromyogram unless the mechanical conditions are also considered.

More physiological conditions, in which, $L_c$ and $Lp$ vary simultaneously, do not lend themselves to graphical constructions. They require computer simulation and will not be pursued here. *The point has already been made in the two examples that EMG cannot be regarded as a predictor of tension, whatever method of description is adopted, unless the influence of muscle length and its time derivative upon the mechanical behaviour are also taken into account.* Under particular circumstances, e.g. a movement of restricted range and speed, an empirical relationship may well be found between EMG and tension or mechanical impulse. We cannot, unfortunately, expect it to be valid if the mechanical conditions are altered. The examples were supposed to apply to a motor unit, but the general conclusions are true for a population of motor units and for a muscle group.

It is possible in limited experimental circumstances to model the behaviour of a muscle group in terms of elastic and contractile elements Wilkie (1950), Cavanagh and Grieve (1970), rather in the manner that the discussion above followed in relation to a motor unit. However, except for the unusual conditions of maximal activation (maximal voluntary effort) or complete re· , the general

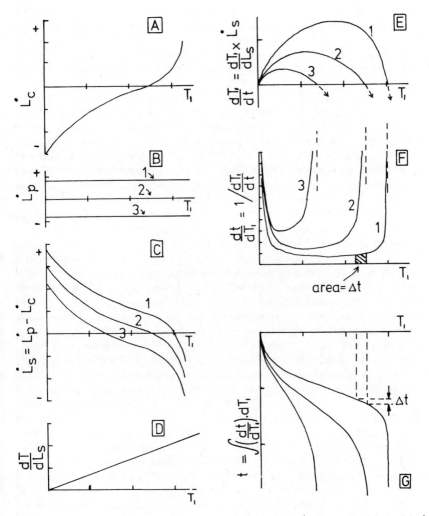

*Fig. 9. Graphical construction of the rise of active tension (without parallel elasticity) during a tetanic contraction at constant rate of stretch (1), isometric (2) or constant rate of shortening of the whole muscle. The same abscisa is used throughout and the symbols are those used in Fig. 6. Ordinates in C are the sum of ordinates in A & B. D represents the stiffness of the series elastic element. The ordinates in E are the product of ordinates in C & D. Ordinates in F are the reciprocal of those in E. Integration of F between two tensions gives the time taken for the tension to rise between these limits, yielding the tension-time curves in G. Note the steeper rise and higher tension reached when the muscle is being stretched (right, G) than when it is shortening (left), without any change in the degree of activation (or electromyogram).*

case has not been explored. In the case of everyday movements calling for moderate levels of activity against a background of posture control, which may possibly involve the differential employment of slow and fast motor units, it is likely that satisfactory models would present enormous complexity. Our simple discussions in the preceding pages is quite sufficient to emphasise that the electromyogram above simply indicates the presence or imminence of mechanical activity. Its significance as regards tension development depends upon a knowledge of the movement and posture and of the intrinsic properties of the muscle group. This latter territory is almost unexplored in both animals and humans as far as natural physiological conditions are concerned. Although no general rules of prediction exist at the moment, the value of a statement about electromyograms in a kinesiological study is clearly enhanced by a further (quantitative) statement as to the posture and accompanying movement since we know that all three are determinants of the tension that is developed.

We see that there are very basic reasons why the electromyogram is incapable of predicting, or correlating with, the tension in a muscle, under the most general conditions of movement. Of course, although the EMG may correlate very closely with mechanical behaviour under particular mechanical conditions in which range and speed of movement are subject to constraints e.g. Bigland & Lippold (1945b), Bouisset et al. (1963), Zuniga & Simons (1969). As more analytical work is done in this area the predictive value of surface or wire electromyography under given conditions will no doubt become better established. At present it seems worthwhile to describe the EMG waveforms as carefully as possible, to state how typical the signals are of the region or muscle group, and to measure the movements of the relevant joints that accompany the signals. The latter measurements in particular considerably modify the conclusions we draw, especially when comparing one pattern with another. For example, if an eccentric and a concentric contraction respectively were associated with the identical electromyograms we could safely conclude that higher muscle tensions accompanied the former. What we are lacking at present is the weighting factor to be given to the EMG according to the observed movement in order that we may calculate the relative charges of tension. The time taken for the tension to rise following a brief burst or onset of EMG is likewise very dependent on the mechanical conditions of muscle length and movement. The discussion of the motor unit model served its purpose while avoiding quantitative expressions. It is not legitimate to assume all motor units are similar in a quantitative sense. Human muscles contain both slow and fast types of motor units and they may be differentially involved in voluntary and reflex movement (Buchtal & Schmalbruch, 1970b). We cannot usefully extend the discussion in our present state of knowledge and must regretfully admit that, whatever empirical laws emerge in special cases, the prediction of mechanical or other parameter from the electromyogram in the general case lies in the future.

**Methods of Describing Phasic Electromyograms**

Whether an original EMG waveform recorded during a movement, or a subjective or a machine-derived description is to be presented, it is salutary to consider how you expect the reader to react to your presentation. To what extent do you consider that the description (or waveform) represents the

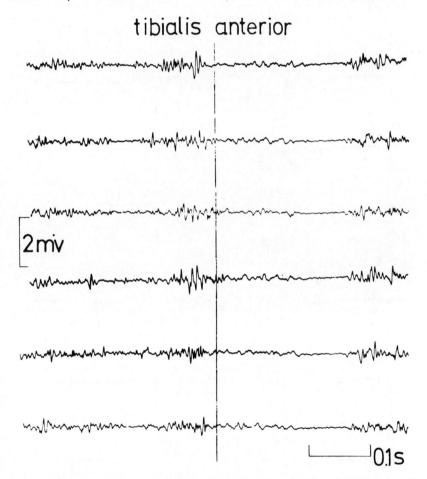

*Fig. 10. Bipolar surface electromyogram from electrodes overlying tibialis anterior. Six consecutive steps are shown from a subject running under familiar conditions at constant speed on a treadmill. Heel strike indicated by a vertical line. No two cycles are the same in detail although it would be pointless to use a method of quantitative description for kinesiological purposes which gave different descriptions at each step.*

electrical activity in the muscle or group? Are you claiming that the description is always applicable, at least to that subject under the same mechanical conditions? If the reader repeats the experiments, even with the same subject, would he obtain the same result? Would a slightly different siting of the electrodes, skin preparation or equipment specification lead to similar or different results? Consideration of all these points is possibly too much to

## hamstrings

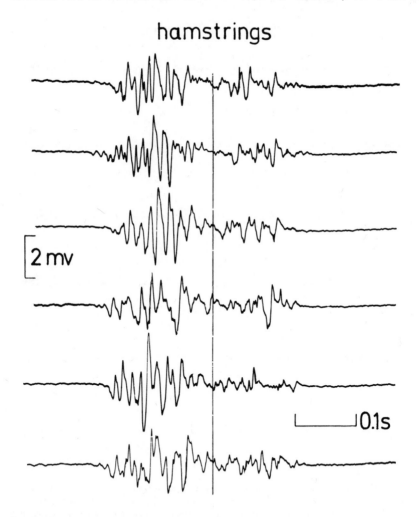

*Fig. 11. Bipolar surface electromyograms of treadmill running from electrodes overlying the hamstring muscles. See Fig. 10 for legend.*

expect in every electromyographic paper but it is surprising that almost no consideration of them is published. The usual practice is to present isolated electromyograms of phasic activity together with a calibration. What is the reader to make of it? A repeat movement does not give rise to an identical electromyogram although it is never certain that the movement has been repeated exactly in the mechanical sense. The presence of activity in a single motor unit close to an electrode during one movement and not in the next is sufficient to alter the detailed form of an electromyogram although the mechanical result of that unit's activity would be completely negligible as far as the sensitivity of the techniques for measuring movement are concerned. Figs. 10 and 11 show sets of consecutive electromyograms obtained from a limb muscle during running at constant speed on a treadmill. The subject, an athlete, was completely familiar with the mill after spending many hours on it and it would be difficult to devise a more stereotyped activity. In spite of this no two cycles repeat themselves exactly. In this state of affairs, the most useful methods of description are those which emphasise the common factors in 'repeat' waveforms.

## Semi-quantitative Assessments.

A common approach to the electromyogram is to assign values to the amplitude (and frequency?) of the trace excursions on a 3- or 4-point scale e.g. none (0), slight (+), moderate (++) and strong (+++). Such assessments are not easy to communicate to a critical reader. A record always contains a background of noise (or if not, the trace line has appreciable thickness). What then is meant by (0) and would (0) have been obtained from an adjacent electrode site? Even the simple approach should contain a description of the electrode placement relative to anatomical landmarks, because the amplitude and form of the signal may both vary rapidly with position of the electrodes. It is also appropriate to give examples of the standards that you have used for ratings. The ratings are more easily obtained for 'steady' electromyograms as may be encountered in some quasi-static postural studies. This book is principally concerned with movements however, and the electromyograms associated with movement are phasic in character. In the latter case, it is very difficult to make a visual assessment and place it on a semi-quantitative basis, even if you furnish examples. Unless some very formal, machine-assisted description can be given (capable of repetition by others and free of the subjective element), it may be best to publish the original waveforms and allow the reader to draw his own conclusions.

Various authors have used a whole series of different descriptions of waveforms as alternatives or in addition to publishing the original. In one case the times at which excursions first exceed and finally fall below fifteen percent of the maximum excursion in a burst are presented. This presentation (Battye & Joseph, 1966) takes no account of the manner in which the burst develops and decays. In spite of its apparently quantitative nature it relies upon a visual judgment, since it would be extremely difficult to programme a computer to recognise definite single instants of onset and decay without also recognising periods of 'chatter' where small excursions follow larger ones and vice versa. Programming to remove the chatter will be equivalent to making a visual judgment. Other authors have attempted to emphasise the general form of the envelope of the waveform either by tracing around it (Sheffield *et al*, 1956) or by stylising the envelope into a series of wedge shapes (Sorbie and Zalter, 1965). Another alternative arises from the use of analogue circuits which first full-wave-rectify the waveform and then smooth the output by means of a bled capacitor. The smoothing circuit imposes a delay in the apparent onset and prolongation in the apparent time of decay. If the time constant is very short,

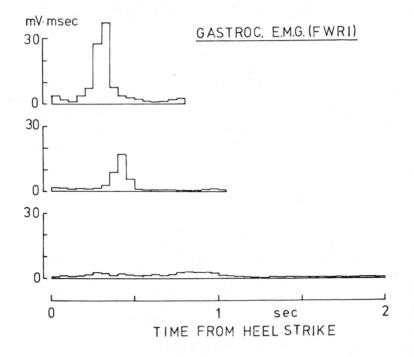

*Fig. 12. A quantitative description of surface electromyograms from gastrocnemic muscle during walking at 3 different speeds. Each 50 msec-period of EMG after heel strike has been quantified by computer analysis of the digitised waveform. In this case the full-wave-rectified integral (FWRI, described in Fig. 15) is shown and should be compared with other measures of the same waveform in Figs. 13 & 14.*

the individual excursions in the waveform are apparent and the envelope's shape becomes obscured. Some sort of smoothing is obviously required, but the influence of a chosen time constant upon the exact quantitative result and especially upon the temporal features, which are such an important part of the description of a phasic electromyogram, are difficult to judge.

## Computer Analysis of Electromyograms

If a numerical description is required, a more versatile approach (and more costly) is to digitise the original waveform before processing. It is then possible to process the same waveforms in various ways.

Three further methods of describing phasic electromyograms, based upon digitised waveforms and computer processing are shown in Figs. 12, 13 and 14.

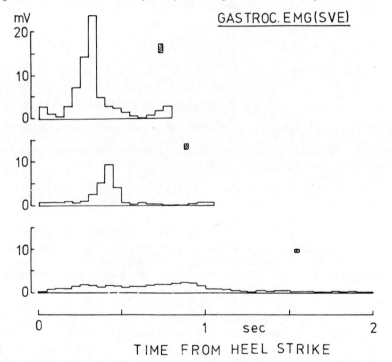

Fig. 13. The summation of voltage excursion (SVE), as described in Fig. 16, of the gastrocnemic signals featured in Figs. 12 & 14. Note the similarity of description to that of the FWRI in Fig. 12. The description is based upon the mean description of 2 consecutive steps. 95% of all SVE descriptions in a particular 50 msec sample of this subject fall within the depth of the shaded bar unless the speed of walk is altered.

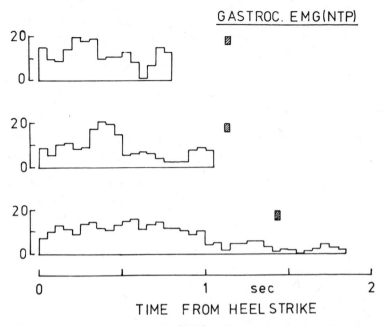

GASTROC. EMG(NTP)

TIME FROM HEEL STRIKE

*Fig. 14. The number of turning points (NTP) in 50 msec samples from the gastrocnemic EMGs featured in Figs. 12 & 13. The description is different in form to the FWRI and SVE descriptions and suggests activity in the muscle (at a low level) at times when the other measure suggest inactivity. The NTP detects low levels of activity but does not emphasise the peaks of activity.*

In these examples, the record has been divided into sample periods of 50 msec and a number obtained by computation on the waveform in each sample. Each method is exact in the sense that the process can be exactly defined, and does not have a subjective element. The discreet samples, however, give rise to discontinuities and the temporal features may be obscured if the sample periods are too extended. A compromise is necessary, since very short samples are affected strongly by the individual features of the waveform.

This sort of discussion of the sampling of envelopes of waveforms emphasises how visually oriented we are when considering the electromyograms i.e. we are not sure what we should do with a quantitative description of a phasic EMG. The three digital techniques will be described in more detail because it was possible with them to consider more carefully the accuracy with which quantitative statements about electromyograms can be made.

Two features of the electromyogram attract the eye. One is the amplitude of the excursions and the other is how frequently they occur. A visual judgment of the 'intensity' of a segment of record, from either surface or wire electrodes, is based upon these features. Since there is at present no special justification for looking 'further than the eye can see' it seems reasonable to use the visual features as the basis for formal definitions of the electromyographic intensity. An exception will be made in the case of the full-wave-rectified integral (FWRI or IEMG) which will also be discussed. Although the eye does not see an integral, several current instruments for quantifying the waveform are based upon it. Even this measure probably arose from a wish to put a number to the shape of a rectified and smoothed waveform. New measures should in any case be related to the tried and familiar measures, but, as far as the description of phasic electromyograms is concerned, the integral has no special merit over any other measure.

Dowling *et al.* (1968) first drew attention to the obvious features of the waveform derived from a population of motor units i.e. to the excursions and their frequency of occurrence, as the basis for a quantitative device. They were particularly concerned with its clinical application with more or less steady state EMGs over periods of many seconds. We are concerned with EMGs recorded during movement and which therefore fluctuate rapidly in intensity. For this reason, what follows differs in detail from that of Willison's group.

Descriptions of EMGs recorded during movement should be capable of following the general changes of pattern within the frequency range of the movement itself or of the forces produced. If the description becomes too concerned with the minutiae of the waveform (at least in biomechanical or kinesiological, rather than neurological, studies), it will be as complex as the original waveform and therefore no advantages will accrue from the derived measure.

The period of the recording is divided up into short sample periods, for each of which a number is to be obtained which reflects the 'intensity' of activity contained within it. In practice, periods of the order of 50 msec duration might be considered which will reflect fluctuations of the EMG that occur at frequencies around 20 Hz. One cannot be dogmatic about the minimum practicable sample periods although it would seem sensible to avoid sampling frequencies that encroach upon the frequency band of the EMG equipment. It is also desirable to select measures of the EMG that give zero quantity in the absence of discernible EMG activity at the level of the noise generated by the tissues and the equipment.

As a starting point in the author's laboratory, electromyograms were digitised at 10 kHz. No appreciable frequency content existed above 5kHz (this was ensured by the presence of filter- circuits), so that the digitised waveform was considered to be free of spurious effects of aliasing and foldback. Under these circumstances, all frequency components of the signal were present. For many purposes (see Fig. 1) heavier filtering could have been employed with the benefit of much lower rates of digitisation. Samples of 50 msec. duration were chosen as the basis for describing the waveform.

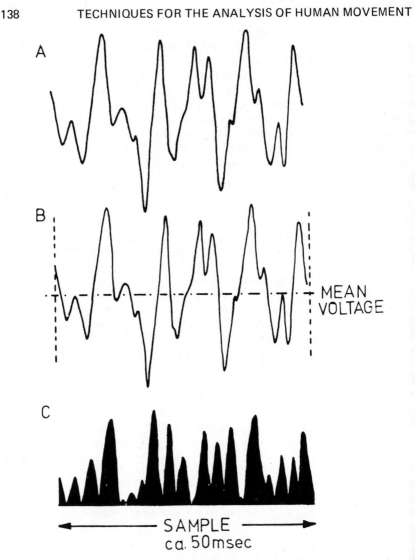

Fig. 15. Showing method of obtaining the full-wave-rectified integral (FWRI). The waveform A is in digital form and analysis is performed by digital computer. The mean voltage in a chosen sample, say 50 msec., of the phasic electromyogram, is determined as shown in B. Finally the area of the curve above the base line, irrespective of size, is computed by trapezoidal rule (typically 5000 digitisations/sec. or more, i.e. 250 trapezoids or more per sample to yield the FWRI. Analogue circuits will also perform rectification and integration. Step B is necessary on each 50 msec sample in digital processing to avoid confusion between low EMG activity and slow baseline drift.

In the first method of description (Grieve & Cavanagh, 1973), the arithmetic mean voltage, i.e. the effective baseline during each consecutive 50 msec was determined. The true full-wave-rectified integral about each baseline was determined by application of the trapezoidal rule to each pair of digitisations in turn throughout the chosen sample (see Fig. 15). It was necessary to establish the baseline separately for each sample rather than choose a common baseline throughout the whole record because slow shifts of the baseline occur which arise because of small movements of the electrodes on the skin surface that cannot be eliminated in general. These shifts do not arise under static conditions. They can be reduced to a minimum by the use of Ag-AqCl reversible electrodes but never eliminated with certainty during vigorous movement. The use of the individual baselines for each sample eliminates the appearance of spurious integrals arising from baseline shift which cannot be otherwise distinguished from genuine EMG integrals at low levels of intensity. The numerical values obtained are referred to as the FWRI (Full-Wave-Rectified-Integral).

The second method consisted of summing the voltage excursions, irrespective of their direction, in each sample period, providing that the excursions exceed a chosen threshold. The computer must be programmed to recognise the turning points in the waveform and calculate the magnitudes of the excursions that they terminate, as illustrated in Fig. 16. The threshold was determined by examination of the amplitude histogram of a signal that was judged to be free of electromyogram i.e. one which only contained noise. The threshold criterion ensured that zero voltage excursion was recorded whenever the subject was judged to be at rest. In practice, the threshold was about 40 microvolt although as little as 5 microvolt is possible with a completely relaxed subject. The measure of the waveform was called the SVE (Summation of Voltage Excursions).

In the process of determining the SVE, the computer had to recognise turning points which terminated excursions that exceeded threshold. It was therefore a simple matter to count the number of turning points in each 50 msec sample, which provided the third measure called the NTP (Number of Turning Points).

Examples of FWRI, SVE and NTP analyses of a few waveforms from a gastrocnemius muscle during locomotion are given in Figs. 12, 13 and 14. Let us now examine these three measures in greater detail. It is obvious from the account of their derivations above, that they are quite distinct and objective measures of the waveforms and there is no reason to expect anything other than empirial relations between them. We may of course have reason to modify that view when we understand more about the mode of operation of muscles and the relationships between events within the muscles and the electromyogram. It would be interesting to learn from the applied psychologists what it is that the electromyographer 'sees' when he examines a phasic recording i.e. a record with rapid fluctuations of intensity made during a movement. Although other opinions doubtless exist, the writer believes that the eye responds principally to the voltage excursions and does not pay as much attention to their frequency of

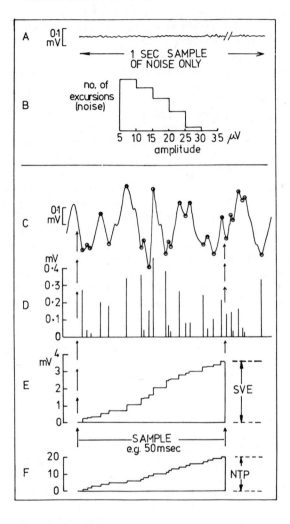

*Fig. 16. Determination of Summation of Voltage Excursion (SVE) and Number of Turning
Points (NTP) of digitised electromyogram.*
*A. Sample of noise (electromyogram judged to be free of muscle activity in relaxed subject).*
*B. Histogram analysis of voltage excursions between turning points in noise. The threshold
for subsequent analysis is chosen (here 35μV) to ensure zero output in absence of EMG. C.
Digitised electromyogram. The computer finds all turning points that terminate excursions
which exceed threshold. These excursions are shown schematically in D, assigned to their
times of termination. The excursions in the sample period are summed to give SVE in E and
the number of turning points are summed to give NTP in F.*

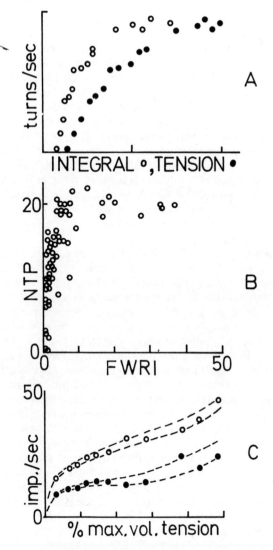

Fig. 17. A: Turning points in 8 second samples of steady isometric surface electromyograms from triceps brachii measured with a Willison-Fitch analyser (Medelec Ltd.) as a function of the integral (open circles) and force at the hand (closed circles), from Troup (1973). B: Relationship between NTP & FWRI of 50 msec samples of surface electromyograms from gastrocnemius during locomotion at 3 speeds (cf. A). C: The maximum and minimum rates of discharge of motoneurones found at various intensitites of contraction in abductor digiti minimi, from Bigland & Lippold (1954a).

occurence. Computer analysis of hundreds of waveforms obtained during locomotion show that the SVE and FWRI in the same 50 msec samples are closely related to each other, i.e. they increase or decrease together. The NTP analysis does not relate to either in this way. Generally speaking, the number of turning points rises very rapidly as the integral increases slightly above zero and does not show a consistent change from the level with further increase of the integral. This behaviour, which the reader may already have discerned by comparing Figs. 12, 13 and 14 is illustrated in Fig. 17b in the case of locomotor i.e. phasic, electromyograms from gastrocnemius. The behaviour is very similar to that found in longer samples of steady state isometric electromyograms reported by Troup and Chapman (1972) (with needle, wire or surface electrodes) and reminiscent of the discharge patterns of motor units that Bigland and Lippold (1954a) reported. To furnish an NTP analysis in addition to one of the others, is to say something extra about the waveform which those concerned with the neural control of the movement rather than the mechanical actions of the muscles may find of great interest.

If the waveform analyses in Figs. 12 and 13 are compared, it can be seen that the SVE or FWRI tell a story that is in close agreement with other authors, i.e. that the gastrocnemius muscle is particularly active at times during the walking cycle when the limb is able to exert a forward and upward thrust upon the trunk. The NTP analysis suggests that the muscle is active at other times during the cycle also, only passing into an almost complete state of rest for a brief period during mid-swing. Similar situations are to be found in all the muscle groups of the lower limb during locomotion (see Fig. 18) and it is safe to assume that they would also arise in other body movements. What are the muscles doing? Possibly we maintain our muscles in states of low activity during voluntary movements instead of resting them even when there is no mechanical demand for their action, in this way holding them in a state of preparedness. Such actions as 'taking up the slack' in a stretched muscle, or some process of rapid servo adjustment spring to mind. These remarks are highly speculative. The original observations need checking with wire as well as surface electrodes because cross talk effects may be contributing to the NTP without affecting the other measures. The evidence is fair, but not conclusive, that there is some sort of activity to be detected in muscles at times when the internal needs of the limb may require attention although external forces are not required. It is clear that the number of turning points is a measure which is worthy of attention in conjunction with either the FWRI or the SVE (but not both).

## Significance of a Computer Description

It is to be hoped that the reader who is contemplating the computer analysis of electromyograms will consider most carefully whether the labour involved (in

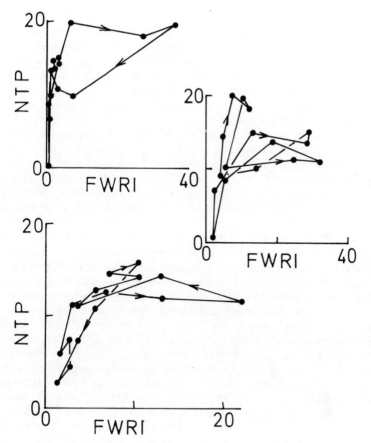

*Fig. 18. Plots of the number of turning points (NTP) in consecutive samples of surface electromyograms during a cycle of locomotion as a function of the corresponding integrals of the samples. Sample period: 50 msec. Top left: gastrocnemius. Right: tibialis anterior. Below: Vastus lateralis. The muscle groups are only 'silent' as indicated by both low integral (FWRI) and low turning points for very short periods in the cycle, prompting the question as to what the muscles are doing at times in the cycle when tension is not demanded of them.*

both software and data handling) justifies the improvements that are to be expected in the accuracy of assessment. Let us start with the assumption that the visual ratings of short samples of an electromyogram (not steady isometric ones) could be made on a 4 point scale in such a way that a group of independent observers would agree on the ratings. Can a computer improve upon this? The important question to be answered is how many points on a scale of

EMG ratings are meaningful, or, alternatively, what level of differences of EMG ratings become statistically significant. To answer this one should, ideally, find a body action which, if repeated, will be accompanied by identical muscle actions. We do not wish to beg the question if we can help it, but it is obvious that we have no reason to suppose that electromyograms *ever* repeat themselves exactly. The way around the difficulty is to adopt a practical approach of studying a highly skilled, repetitive moment (e.g. walking at a steady speed). If electromyograms are ever to repeat themselves, they will do so under these conditions. Put another way, if the quantitative description of the EMG does vary from step to step under these conditions, we would be inclined to say that the differences were of no consequence from a kinesiological point of view and that the numerical analysis should be 'rounded-off' until it is the same for each step.

Suppose we record electromyograms from a subject walking at various steady speeds. Two consecutive cycles will be considered in each case and each cycle divided into 50 msec samples, starting with heel-strike. The averages $\bar{y}_n$ of corresponding samples $x_n$ and $x'_n$ in the two cycles are determined and the regression of $x_n$ and $x'_n$ values against their $\bar{y}_n$ values for all the samples calculated. The $x_n$ and $x'_n$ are scattered about the regression line. The distance of 1.96 times the root mean square residual gives the limits above and below the regression line in which 95% of all such samples are expected. This tells us what confidence we may place in the EMG description which is an average of the descriptions from the first and second cycles. The analyses in Figs. 12, 13 and 14 are mean descriptions obtained in this way and the small vertical bars on Figs. 12 and 14 represent 1.96 times the residuals. If the sample values differ by that amount we can say that there is only a five percent probability that the differences arose by chance. We can use the same criterion to decide how many points can be used in a scale of EMG ratings. The more vigorous the EMG e.g. as walking speed is increased, the larger the residuals about the regression lines mentioned above. To take this into account, the maximum sample number obtained in a computer description of a phasic electromyogram (peak of intensity) may be divided by (1.96 x residual). We obtain a number whose integer is the effective number of points on a scale that can be used to describe the waveform and which would lead, in 95 repeated cycles of movement out of 100, to the same numerical description of it.

Surface electromyograms from eleven muscle groups were examined at twelve speeds of walking in one subject. Under the best conditions that were found, the SVE and FWRI samples were both capable of being represented within 95% levels of confidence on 15 point scales (at least 8-point in half the cases studied), which is a great improvement upon any subjective visual assessment. In a few cases, the differences between corresponding samples in the consecutive cycles were greater so that only a 4 or 5 point scale was usable. The NTP measurements produced repeatable patterns on an 8 point scale at best (5 point in more than half the cases) and on a 3 point scale in the worst case. In many cases therefore it appears that a computer assessment is capable of finer discrimination than can be achieved by eye. The improvement is not so startling in some instances that the case for using a computer is overwhelming. The ability of the machine to crunch numbers is impressive, but that is not the point. What we must establish is the level at which we can communicate meaningfully about electromyograms. The ability of the machine to produce a four figure number does not mean that it should be used unless all digits are significant in a biological sense.

The comments above really refer to the fineness of description that is meaningful when considering signals that are recorded at a particular electrode site. This is useful, for example, in the type of experiment in which the mechanical conditions are changed systematically throughout a series of movements. Slightly different considerations apply when making a general statement about the use of this or that muscle group in a class of activity, e.g. in a golf drive or a stereotyped industrial task. It is unlikely that the reader will be as concerned with the absolute intensities (millivolt, etc.) as with the temporal pattern. It is most important to be able to attribute the activity to a particular group. Figure 18 shows SVE analyses obtained from simultaneous bipolar surface recordings over the gluteal region. In absolute terms, it is obvious that the strength of signals depends very much upon the actual electrode sites. When the results are expressed in normalised form i.e. the percentage of the total activity found in each sample, it is seen that the signals have approximately the same temporal form. They may therefore be attributed to the activity of the hip abductors of the gluteal region with much more confidence than could the signal from one site without this preliminary check. When this sort of check is applied to simultaneous electromyograms from the shank it is found that the signal is very sensitive to electrode position because so many muscles are closely placed with different tasks to perform. The same is true of signals from electrodes on the medial surface of the thigh. The clue to the presence of different sources of the electromyogram is to be found in the comparison of simultaneous records and analyses from grids of electrodes. The computer is ideal for this purpose because the normalised result is as easily obtained as the analysis in absolute units. Making such comparisons visually is extremely difficult from the raw waveforms because the eye does not easily compare signals of very different amplitude when they are presented on the same time-scale.

## Combining Data on Electromyographic Signals and Movements

It was argued above that it is more meaningful to consider both the movement and the electromyograph together rather than publish the latter alone because the tension in a muscle (which is the elusive quantity of principal interest) in a given state of activity is strongly dependent upon the muscle's length and its velocity.

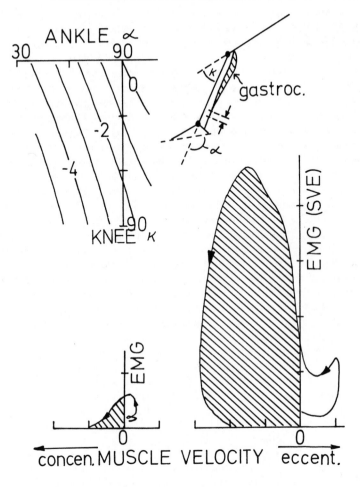

Fig. 19. Above: Lines of constant length of gastrocnemius muscle, drawn on a plot of ankle angle against knee angle, as determined from cadaveric observations. The sketch on the left shows the manner of creating a gap in the tendon for purposes of measurement while the postures of the cadaveric joints are altered systematically.

Below: The diagram on the left is a plot of the quantified electromyogram (SVE) from gastrocnemius as a function of muscle velocity during a cycle of slow walking. The velocity was determined from cine analysis and from the data above. The shaded area represents concentric activity in which the muscle acts as a prime mover. The muscle commences activity as a stabiliser and the activity decays as soon as the stretching has been checked. The diagram on the right was obtained at a high walking speed. Not only is there much more electromyographic activity but the bulk of the activity occurs when the muscle is acting as a prime mover, in strong contrast to the behaviour on the left (from data of Cavanagh, 1972).

It is possible, at least in some muscles, to determine how the distance between attachments varies as a function of joint posture. This may be done by examining cadavers in which unwanted tendons have been sectioned so that the joints are free to move. The distances between the cut ends of a chosen tendon are then measured as a function of joint angles, e.g. both ankle and knee joints in the case of gastrocnemius. The results of photographic or goniometric studies may then be used to predict how the length of a particular muscle was changing during an experiment in the living subject. Proceeding in this manner, it is possible to express the electromyogram as a function of muscle length or muscle velocity.

An example of the use of gastrocnemius for this purpose is given in Fig. 19, due to Cavanagh (1972). In this example, which illustrates the use of the muscle at a slow and a fast speed of walking, it was seen in Fig. 12 and 13 that the intensity of electromyogram in gastrocnemius increases dramatically as the speed of walking increases. The use of gastrocnemius to assist with the extensor thrust during locomotion is of little importance in a very slow walk. The muscle is activated while it is being stretched (which is an economical way of developing tension between the calcaneum and the femur) and, as soon as the stretch has been checked and shortening begins, the muscle relaxes again. This is in marked contrast to the behaviour at high speed. The active muscle is initially being stretched. Since both the intensity of electromyogram and the rate of stretch are greater than at low speed, it is reasonable to assume that much greater tensions are exerted at the higher speed. It would also appear that the body is intent on getting as large a mechanical impulse as possible from the muscle because the electromyogram increases still further while shortening takes place, even though it is relatively uneconomical when compared with the mechanical condition of the initial activation. This later phase of concentric contraction is almost absent at low speeds of walking.

## References

BATTYE, C.K. & JOSEPH, J. (1966). An investigation by telemetering of the activity of some muscles in walking. *Med. Biol. Engng.,* **4**, 125-135.

BASMAJIAN J.V. (1968). The present status of electromyographic kinesiology. In J. Wartenweiler, E. Jokl & M. Hebbelinck (Eds.), *Medicine & Sport 2, Biomechanics.* Basel & New York: Karger.

BIGLAND, B. & LIPPOLD, O.C.J. (1954a). Motor unit activity in the voluntary contraction of human muscle. *J. Physiol.*, **125**, 322-335.

BIGLAND, B. & LIPPOLD, O.C.J. (1954b). The relation between force, velocity and integrated electrical activity in human muscle. *J. Physiol.*, **123**, 214-224

BLACK, W.W. (1971). *An Introduction to On-line Computers.* London: Gordon & Breach.

BOUISSET, S., DEMINAL, J. & SOULA, C. (1963). Relation entre l'accelera-tion d'un raccourcissement musculair et l'activite electromyographique integree. *J. Physiol.*, (Paris) **55**, 203.

BUCHTAL, F., & SCHMALBRUCH, H. (1970a). Contraction times and fibre types in intact human muscle. *Acta Physiol. Scand.,* **79**, 435-452.

BUCHTAL, F., & SCHMALBRUCH, H. (1970b). Contraction times of twitches evoked by H-reflexes. *Acta Physiol. Scand.,* **80**, 378-382.

BUCTAL F., GULD C., & ROSENFALCK, P. (1957). Multi-electrode study of the territory of a motor unit. *Acta Physiol. Scand.,* **39**, 83-104.

CAVANAGH, P.R. (1972). Patterns of muscular action and movement associa-ted with the range of speeds used in normal human locomotion. Ph.D. thesis. University of London.

CAVANAGH, P.R. & GRIEVE, D.W. (1970). The release and partitioning of mechanical energy during a maximal effort of elbow flexion. *J. Physiol.,* **210**, 44-45.

CHAFFIN, D.B. (1969). Surface electromyography frequency analysis as a diagnostic tool. *J. Occup. Med.,* **11**, 109-115.

CLOSE, R.I. (1972). Dynamic properties of mammalian skeletal muscles. *Physiol. Rev.,* **52**, 129-197.

DOWLING, M.H., FITCH, P. & WILLISON, R.G. (1968). A special purpose digital computer (Biomac 500) used in the analysis of the human electro-myogram. *Electroenceph. Clin. Neurophysiol.,* **25**, 570.

GORDON, A.M., HUXLEY, A.F. & JULIAN, F.J. (1966). The variation in isometric tension with sarcomere length in vertebrate muscle fibres. *J. Physiol.,* **184**, 170.

GRIEVE, D.W. & CAVANAGH, P.R. (1973). The quantitative analysis of phasic electromyograms. In J.E. Desmedt (Ed.), *New developments in electro-myography and Clinical neurophysiology.* Vol. 2. Basel: Karger.

JONSSON, B. (1968). Wire electrodes in electromyographis kinesiology. In J. Wartenweiler, E. Jokl. & M. Hebbelinck (Eds.), *Medicine & Sport 2, Biomechanics.* Basel & New York: Karger.

LIPPOLD, O.C.J. (1952). The relation between integrated action potentials in a human muscle and its isometric tension. *J. Physiol.,* **117**, 492-499.

NIGHTINGALE, A. (1957). A study of the electrical activity in normal resting and active human muscle. Ph.D. thesis. University of London.

PATTLE, R.E. (1971). The external action potential of a nerve or muscle fibre in an extended medium. *Phys. Med. Biol.,* **16**, 673-685.

RACK, P.N.H. & WESTBURY, D.R. (1969). The effects of length and stimulus rate on tension in the isometric cat soleus muscle. *J. Physiol.*, **204**, 443-460.

SATO, M., HAYAMI, A. & SATO, H. (1965). Differential fatiguability between the one- and two-joint muscles. *J. Anthrop. Soc. Nippon,* **73**, 82-90.

SHEFFIELD, F.J., GERSTEN, J.W. & MASTELLONE, A.F. (1956). Electromyographic study of the muscles of the foot in normal walking. *Amer. J. Phys. Med.,* **35**, 223-236.

SORBIE, C. & ZALTER, R. (1965). Bioengineering studies of the forces transmitted by joints. Part I. The pahsic relationship of the hip muscles in walking. In R.M. Kenedi (Ed.), *Biomechanics and Related Bio-engineering Topics.* Oxford: Pergamon.

TROUP, J.D.G. & CHAPMAN, A.E. (1972). Analysis of the waveform of the electromyograph using the analyser described by Fitch (1967). *Electromyography,* **12**, 325-345.

WILKIE, D.R. (1950). The relation between force and velocity in human muscle. *J. Physiol.,* **110**, 249-280.

ZUNIGA, E.N. & SIMONS, D.G. (1969). Non-linear relationship between averaged electromyogram potential and muscle tension in normal subjects. *Arch. Phys. Med. Reh.,* **50**, 613-619.

# 5

# INSTRUMENTS FOR FORCE MEASUREMENT

Section

# INSTRUMENTS FOR FORCE MEASUREMENT

by J.P. PAUL.

## Applications

In the assessment of certain athletic performances such as weight lifting, and in the ergonomic assessment of normal labour, it is obviously necessary to measure the force exerted by man on his environment. In other situations the necessity is less obvious but none the less vital. In the clinical context the amputee suffers a loss not only in skeletal structure but also in muscle (i.e. power source), load bearing surface, (feet and hands), and information, (limb position and attitude, grip, texture, temperature etc.) To analyse the energy transfers between limb segments during activity and to measure the forces transmitted at the interface between the prosthesis and amputee requires knowledge of the externally applied force actions. In the same way, to measure the degree of improvement in the locomotion of an arthritic patient after an operation for the fitting of an artificial replacement joint, one useful technique is the measurement of the force transmitted between ground and foot on the affected and unaffected sides. In the field of ergonomics, transducers must effectively be used to measure the forces which an operator can exert in defined directions on control levers and the variation of this force capability with position of the control relative to his body. Similarly, tests have been performed to assess men's capacity for lifting weights and the preferred lifting techniques which should be adopted (Whitney). In athletic performance, assessment of specific features can be greatly assisted by measurement of the relevant forces. As examples one may consider the acceleration of the sprinter starting from the blocks, where transducers incorporated in the blocks give valuable information; the effect of the push-off in assessment of jumping performance and the forces exerted at the hands or feet of a weight lifter during the cycle. Indications of the importance of different muscle groups can only be inferred from a knowledge of the turning actions they require to exert at the neighbouring joints. For instance, consider the leg shown in Fig. 1 during walking on a level surface. Depending on the direction of the ground to foot force it will tend to extend or flex the knee joint and the magnitude of the turning action can be measured during a cycle so

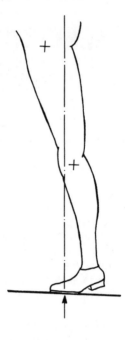

*Fig. 1. Lateral view of the leg of a walking test subject showing the instantaneous position of the line of action of the resultant ground to foot force.*

that, if this activity had to be improved, the relative importance of the knee flexors and extensors could be gauged.

Considering also the frontal view of the leg as in Fig. 2, it is obvious that the line of action passes close to the axis of the ankle joint, medial to the knee joint, and very much medial to the hip joint. Thus, for stable walking, little inversion-eversion activity is required at the ankle but a significant moment has to be exerted in adduction-abduction at the knee. The direction of this moment must increase the force on the medial condyles of the knee corresponding to tension on the lateral ligamentous structure. Again, at the hip, since the line of action of the resultant forces passes well medial to the joint axis, substantial activity of the abductor muscles of the hip will be necessary for stability.

It is interesting to note that necessary muscular activity can be inferred from mechanical diagrams of this type whereas myo-electric studies of themselves convey little information about mechanical actions since corresponding signals are recorded whether the muscle is contracting or being extended against resistance and, in cases of antagonistic muscle activity, the direction of the effective loading action is unknown. If measurement of external force is

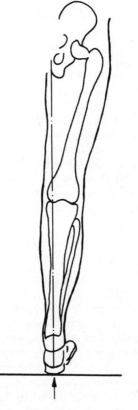

*Fig. 2. View from the rear of the leg of a walking test subject showing the instantaneous position of the line of action of resultant ground to foot force.*

undertaken in conjunction with measurement of limb segment configuration, then, in addition to the moment recording described previously, one can infer information on the development or absorption of energy by the muscles of the leg.

It should be noted that it is not possible to infer this information from kinematic movement studies only, whether the information be acquired by goniometers, by cine or television cameras. The reasons for this are complex. Firstly, one would require to determine the mass of the individual body segments, which can be done with great difficulty for a particular experiment or which can be inferred with questionable accuracy from collected figures of averages of mass properties based on total weight of the subject and the length of the segment. These would have to be known for every segment of the body and one would then require to determine the linear and angular accelerations in all directions of all components. To determine accelerations from measurements of displacement is a particularly inaccurate mathematical process in which the errors may easily exceed the magnitude of the quantity being estimated. An additional and more potent factor is that where the body is supported on two feet the determination of the acceleration forces does not allow the determination of the ground-foot forces, hence in fact the configuration is technically termed "statically indeterminate". This can be very easily demonstrated if one stands with the feet separated by any distance either forwards or sideways. It is possible to tense the leg musculature to try and bring the feet together against the frictional resistance of the floor and obviously, as one does this, one varies the resultant force between ground and foot. If this resultant force can be altered by the action of the musculature it is obvious that no calculations taking account only of the masses and accelerations of body parts can give a true result. It is necessary to have instruments which will determine the load actions of each foot separately.

**Quantities to be Measured**

The early investigators of locomotion concentrated their attention on the major movements, that is the forward progression of the body and the movements of the limbs in the sagittal plane. Studies of locomotion show that the lateral movements of the trunk and the rotational ones are equally important in characterising performance and the force system relating to locomotion must be considered as three dimensional. To measure the component forces between ground and foot will therefore require a measuring system having three recording channels. The position of the line of action of the force is critically important since the resultant moments at joints depend on the magnitude of the force and the offset of line of action from the joint axis. For complete information therefore a dynamometer must be able to measure the position through which the line of action of the resultant force acts (see Fig. 3). This might correspond to the offsets (a) and (b) from the axis of the instrument of the position through which the resultant force acts. The three components of force together with these two dimensions do not however suffice completely to define load actions. This can be exemplified by the situation of someone standing on one heel-tip or toe-tip and rotatating about a vertical axis. There will be a frictional moment at the point of support and this moment transmitted through the contact area is the sixth and final quantity necessary to define load actions. The position at which the foot will lie on a dynamometer can never or can rarely be defined in advance and this moment is therefore usually defined as a moment about the central or reference axis of the dynamometer. The moment about the reference axis will obviously comprise three parts:

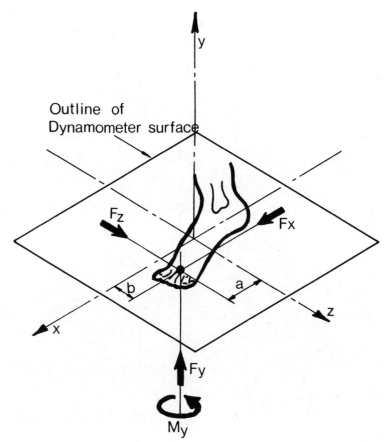

*Fig. 3. Force actions transmitted from ground to foot. Three force components $F_x$ $F_y$ $F_z$ two dimensions a, b defining the position of a resultant vertical force: moment $M_y$ about a vertical access through the area of a foot contact.*

1. The moment My about the centre of the area of contact.
2. Medio lateral force times distance (a)
3. The anterior-posterior force times the distance (b).

Similarly the offset of the position of the resultant force can be measured as an output of the quantity itself or can be signalled as the moment about the horizonal reference axis. Not all force plate dynamometers are equipped to measure these six quantities and studies are performed on types instrumented to

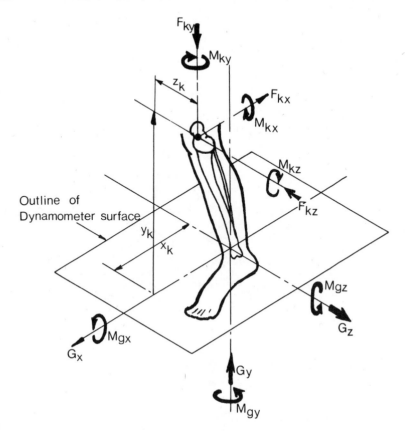

*Fig. 4. "Free body diagram" of the lower leg showing the external forces exerted by the ground and the internal load actions transmitted by the structures at the knee. There will also be gravity and acceleration force actions corresponding to the mass of the foot and the shank, although these are actually negligible during the stance phase.*

measure one or more of these for particular purposes. To illustrate the use of an instrument of this type Fig. 4 shows a free body diagram of a leg up to the knee supported by a force plate which measures all six quantities. If the position of the knee joint is defined in co-ordinates $x_k$, $y_k$, $z_k$ and the effect of the mass of the shank, foot and footwear can be neglected, the resultant force components transmitted between the shank and the thigh are of course $G_x$, $G_y$ and $G_z$ as shown. Note that these are the resultant load actions, the forces in the internal structure of the leg, the tendons and ligaments and joints will be quite different.

The flexion-extension moment will be

$$M_{kz} = M_{Gz} + G_y \times x_k - G_x \times y_k$$

The adduction-abduction moment will be

$$M_{kx} = M_{Gx} + G_z \times y_k - G_y \times z_k$$

and the moment about a vertical axis through the knee joint will be

$$M_{ky} = M_{Gy} + G_x \times z_k - G_z \times x_k.$$

Obviously, without the comprehensive information obtainable only from a six quantity dynamometer these load actions cannot be fully specified. Equally of course information must be acquired to define the position of the joint in question, in this case, the knee. This will usually require the use of two cine or television cameras to record the three coordinates.

**Dynamometer Design**

Force is a difficult quantity to measure and it can be done in two basic ways:-

1. Balance the force so that it causes no displacement of the surface to which it is applied and measure the balancing effect. The balancing effect may be produced by compressing a spring, by an electromagnetic or electrostatic effect or by hydraulic or pneumatic loading.
2. The deformation produced in an elastic system may be measured.

System 2 is usually employed for forceplate systems for ground to foot force measurements and it is of course necessary to limit the deflection of the instrument under load, since a normal person can detect the small difference in deflection, for instance, between a concrete and a timber floor. It is suggested that 1/1000 of an inch should be the maximum deformation. This is however closely related to the dynamic performance of the instrument and its ability to record faithfully forces whose magnitude and direction are changing rapidly. Any elastic structure has several natural frequencies of vibration depending on the direction of the movement and whether it is linear or rotational. In simple terms the natural frequency N vibrations per second is related by equation (1) to the mass of the top plate and other vibrating parts, M Kg, and the elastic stiffness of the restraint, E Newtons per metre deflection or $E^1$ kilograms force per metre deflection.

$$N = \frac{1}{2\pi.} \sqrt{\frac{E}{M}} \quad \dots \dots \dots \dots \dots \dots . (1)$$

or

$$N = \frac{1}{2\pi} \sqrt{\frac{E^1 \ 9.81}{M}}$$

Usually the structure of a forceplate includes some form of 'damping' or energy absorbing characteristics, like the dampers on an automobile suspension. The effect of this is to reduce the magnitude of vibrations more quickly, as shown in Fig. 5. The appearance on a test record of vibrations due to the forceplate is undesirable but the use of heavy damping will make the instrument unsuitable for measuring rapidly changing forces.

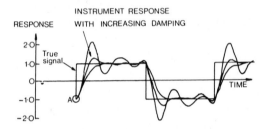

*Fig. 5. Response characteristics of instruments showing the effect of increasing damping. If the true signal is rectangular in form as shown the response of the instrument may show oscillation and phase lag as indicated.*

Design of the instrument will inevitably involve compromise between the various design considerations as follows:-

1.  Maximum mechanical stiffness so that the test subject is not aware of deflection on his foot.
2.  Suitable sensitivity of measuring channels. In this connection it should be noted that for instance the medio lateral force component may frequently be as small as 5% of the vertical component yet its effect on load actions at the hip can be considerable because of the lever arm (equal to leg length) through which it acts. 1% accuracy for instance in measurement of this component of force must therefore imply that it is measured with an accuracy of 1 in 2000 referred to the vertical force component.
3.  The natural frequency of vibration of the force plate in any mode must be high relative to a typical force pattern produced by the activity to be measured on sensitive force transducers.

Force transducers which have been utilised by experimenters have been of various types. Most frequent is the use of electrical resistance strain gauges to measure the surface strain occurring on a suitably designed mechanical component. Usually several gauges are connected in bridge circuits so that instead of signalling the surface strain on the link they will together give a signal corresponding to one of the load actions it is wished to measure independent of the effect of other load actions. In some cases semi-conductor strain gauges have been used because of their larger strain sensitivity factors which give advantages in greater signal unit deformation. The advantage from using semi-conductor strain gauges however is not as great as one would imagine from the fact that the strain sensitivity factor may be 50 times that of an electrical resistance gauge. A much smaller margin of advantage results since the current carrying capacity is much lower. Other difficulties arise also due to increased sensitivity to temperature and also due to change in the sensitivity factor with temperature. When such gauges are connected into bridge circuits it is possible to apply external measured loads to the device in order to produce a calibration curve. Ideally this will be linear and show no effects of hysteresis in the range of loads normally to be measured. Because of errors in the geometry of the force plate, in the placing of the gauges or their strain sensitivity or electrical resistance it will generally be found that a given load action will produce a small signal indicating that another load action is present. These "cross-sensitivities" can be troublesome but their effect may usually be reduced by careful adjustment of the electrical circuit characteristics and also by taking particular care with the mechanical construction. Some users frequently find it satisfactory to recognise that these factors exist and take account of them in the interpretation of the results.

Other types of measuring system measure the mechanical deflection of a structural component by inductive or capacitive electric transducers or by optical methods.

Generally electrical transducers are employed and it should be noted that the characteristics of the force plate itself together with its transducers have to be considered in relation to the other electrical instruments used in conjunction, for example, the power supply to the electrical transducers, the amplifiers used on the output signal and the recorder system, whether it gives a graphical record of the variation with the load action with time, or produces in digital form the values of the load action at predetermined time intervals. Inevitably the characteristics of the overall system will differ from those of the dynamometer itself. For instance, unless the output of the electrical supply to the transducer is stabilised, variation in the main supply voltage or in battery energy sources may give rise to apparent differences in calibration factors from instant to instant or day to day. Similarly, the effect of an amplifier on the electrical output signal will depend on its frequency response and the corresponding phase lag in its output signal. The effective gain and lag will depend on the characteristics of the input signal. Usually an amplifier will be connected to a graphical recording instrument and the limiting factor in the complete system will be the natural frequency of this instrument. The natural frequency of pen and some galvanometer recorders can be quite low and there is no point in building a force-plate dynamometer of a high natural frequency and then using a recording instrument of inferior frequency response.

In all cases it is advisable when the system has been set up to conduct direct calibrations between the quantity to be measured and the output of the recording system both on a static and on a dynamic basis. Otherwise one may be completely deluded and unaware of limitations in the response characteristics of the instrumentation.


**Types of Dynamometer**

There are basically five different types of Dynamometer possible, each with its own particular application and each with its own limitations.

1.   Large area forceplates are those on which both feet can rest simultaneously and which can be used therefore measurements of the total load transmitted by both feet together. Measurement of this type has been used by Dr. R.J. Whitney, Medical Research Council Laboratories in London, where he was investigating the lifting action in men, with a view to specifying optimum body configuration for particular tasks. Such a plate can be used for the measurement of forces on individual feet by arranging that the contralateral foot is supported by the surrounding surface and not by the dynamometer itself. This, of course, limits its use but it can be used for locomotion analyses provided the path of the test subject is suitably oriented. It has the virtue that forces can be measured for more than one foot contact in succession.

2.   The two-track dynamometer system involves two separate tracks generally several metres long arranged so that the subject can easily walk with one foot making contact always with one of the tracks while the other is supported by its own particular track. Because of the length of this track system, it is easy to obtain successive foot forces for the several strides. Instruments of this type are capable of giving signals of vertical component force and sometimes also for the force in the direction of progression. There are none known to this author which give more information. One disadvantage of a system of this type is that the subject must be constrained to walk with feet astride so that they do not stray onto the track for the contralateral foot.

3.   The single-step dynamometer is a form which is usually rectangular, approximately 50 cm x 36 cm, so that a walking individual may make

contact with one foot only on the plate at a time and it is not too difficult for him to ensure that the entire foot contacts the forceplate on the test occasion. If the force exerted by a second foot is required, another dynamometer is placed at a suitable distance in front and to one side. It is theoretically possible to obtain a number of successive footfalls by installing several dynamometers but usually the experimental difficulty of getting the test subject's feet to contact each forceplate individually limits the number installed to two. Instruments of this type usually have the facility for complete measurement of all six quantities defining the force system acting on one foot and, on the next instrument, the six pertaining to the contact of the next foot. An extension of this type of forceplate is the starting block dynamometer where the external force developed by an athlete at the start of a sprint can be measured for one foot only, and generally for a limited number of force components at the commencement of sprint running.

4.  Special footwear. Ideally the test subject should carry force measuring equipment around with him and allow the measurement of the forces at each and every foot contact for both feet. This has not so far been proven possible although instruments have been developed to measure some of the quantities pertaining to the resultant force transmitted. The disadvantage generally of this philosophy of measurement is the thickness of sole required and the additional weight in the footwear which results in the gait characteristics of the individual being altered from what it is desired to measure.

5.  Prosthesis dynamometer. Where the locomotion of a leg amputee is being analysed, it is convenient to instal a dynamometer as part of the structure of the artificial limb. Such dynamometer can give signals corresponding to the full six-component description of the loading action and can be so designed as to add little weight to the limb itself. These devices are usually used with connections to the recording apparatus formed by trailing or suspended wires. Although this is cumbersome, it is frequently found to be more satisfactory than the complications which would result from the use of, for instance, radiotelemetry or pocket tape recorders to acquire the data.

No description of forceplate dynamometers would be complete without reference to that of Amar whose "Trottoir Dynamographique" described in 1916. This instrument had a mechanical measuring system in which spring deflection under load operated appropriate indicators. The quantities measured were vertical sideways and backward force components only. There was no provision for the measure of forward force components or moment actions about any of the reference axes. This instrument was used principally in investigations of the locomotion of amputees using artificial limbs, and the findings were used to suggest design improvements.

Elftman in 1938 reported results obtained from locomotion tests on a forceplate of his design. The assembly carried two plates, one sliding on ball bearings on top of the other against spring resistance, and the force components exerted were measured by the deflection of elastic systems and recorded by cinecamera. There was no provision for the measurement of the moment exerted between ground and foot about a vertical axis through the contact area.

As part of a major exercise aimed at acquiring basic information of mechanics of locomotion at the Berkeley campus of the University of California, D.M. Cunningham and G.W. Brown designed a six-component dynamometer of Type 3, using electrical resistance strain gauges connected in bridge circuits, and in fact this instrument was the first to produce performance which could be considered satisfactory in terms of modern measuring systems. This design has formed the basis for many others in use in several parts of the world and it is appropriate therefore to describe it. As can be seen in Fig. 6 its basic form comprises a cast aluminium top plate mounted by four tubular columns onto a baseplate sitting on adjustable feet on a recess in the ground surface. Each column carried 12 longitudinally mounted electrical resistance strain gauges and these were connected in bridge circuits to give outputs of three components of resultant force and the moments about the three perpendicular axes through the centre of the top plate. In use, horizontal plane vibrations of the top plate gave troublesome signals superimposed on the actual records and a special viscous damping system was installed to alleviate this. Forceplates of basically this type with minor modifications have been used by Harper, Warlow and Clarke at the Buildings Research Station and also by the University of Strathclyde Bioengineering Unit. Basically this forceplate is approximately 20" x 15" so that it is quite possible to measure the force from a single contact of one foot. The strain gauge bridges were energised by direct current and the outputs were amplified before feeding to pen recorders. There is no information available on the dynamic characteristics of the amplifiers or recorders. By the use of semi conductor strain gauge on the columns and sensitive galvanometer recorders, Paul and Morrison of the University of Strathclyde were able to record the output signals directly on a sensitive galvanometer recorder without preamplification. The galvanometer natural frequency was 100 Hz.

Dynamometers of type 1 have been described by Skorecki and by Rydell. The former is installed in the Centre for Hip Surgery at Wrightington in Lancashire and is routinely used to analyse the difference in vertical component of force exerted by the feet of patients with joint disease. Records are taken before and after surgery to replace the hip joint and the test records give a quantitative assessment of the alteration in the locomotion of the patient. Generally considerably greater load bearing can be achieved on the affected limb after replacement of the joint by an implanted prosthetic device. The basic

Fig. 6. Exploded view of force plate constructed at University of California Berkeley.
Reproduced from Proc. Soc. Exp. Stress Analysis Volume 9. 1952.

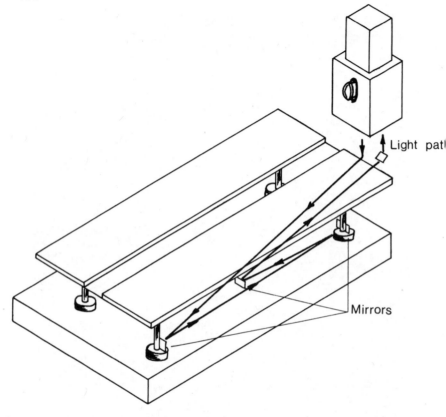

Light path

Mirrors

*Fig. 7. Schematic view of gait machine designed by Dr. J. Skorecki and installed at the Hospital for Hip Surgery at Wrightington.*

structure of this instrument is shown in Fig. 7 and as can be seen, the transducers at each end incorporated into the beam supports comprise a mechanical system using optical methods to amplify the small displacement of the spring and damper system. This is a particularly useful feature in that the maintenance required and the calibration checks required of a system of this type are minimal. Rydell's instrument is of basically the same type but the transducers for vertical force measurement are 'Bofors' force cells in which the small deflection of a mechanical system is measured electrically. This forceplate also has provision for the measurement of the force component acting along the length of the track. It was originally installed in the Department of Orthopaedics at the University of Gothenburg but is now in the Karolinska Institute at Stockholm.

Several forms of dynamometer of type 3 exist in addition to the ones already discussed, one which Dr. A. H. Burstein of Case Western Reserve University in Cleveland installed in his laboratory and also at Moss Rehabilitation Hospital in Philadelphia. Another specimen of this type is incorporated in the walkway assembly at the limb fitting centre at Valenton near Paris. A six quantity dynamometer of this type is now marketed by the Kistler Company and is shown in Fig. 8. The transducers are piezo electric crystals and it is claimed that the minimum natural frequency of vibration is greater than 200 Hz.

*Fig. 8. Compact force plate designed and marketed by Messrs. Kistler.*

Load measuring sandals were designed at the Royal Aeronautical Establishment in Farnborough to the specification of Dr. John T Scales. Typical sandals of this type are shown in Fig. 9. In this, special rubber compound forming the complete base of the sandal is sandwiched between two metallic grids. Compression of the rubber due to normal force alters the electrical capacitance between the grids in a measurable fashion and this signal is transmitted by a radio telemetry set incorporated in the heel of the sandal to a remote recorder. The desirable feature of this instrument is the lack of constraint for the test subject. Unfortunately it is able to give only the resultant force normal to the walking surface. Sandals of a similar type have been developed at the Biomechanics Institute at Montpellier France under the direction of Professor P Rabischong. In these it is possible to introduce cells to measure the tangential force but, as yet, it is not possible to measure all six quantities necessary to define the load action. Carlsoo in Stockholm has conducted experiments on patients wearing special shoes which were equipped with three transducers whose output defined completely the force normal to the supporting surface in respect of magnitude and position of its line of action relative to the shoe. Unfortunately, there was no provision for measurement of shear force.

*Fig. 9. "Load measuring sandal" designed for Dr. J. Scales of the Royal National Orthopaedic Hospital Stanmore by the Royal Aircraft Establisshment at Farnborough.*

Fig. 10. Load measuring dynamometer installed in lower limb prosthesis.

Prosthesis dynamometers were another of the design features introduced to the analysis field by Cunningham and Brown in California. Instruments of their basic type have been used at many centres and the one used at the University of Strathclyde is shown in Fig. 9. In addition to the force measurement, an electrical potentiometer is used to measure knee angle and the outputs of these seven quantities allow the assessment of the resultant force actions transmitted at the knee and at the hip. These quantities are very sensitive to the alignment of the prostheses and govern the effective use which the amputee can make of it.

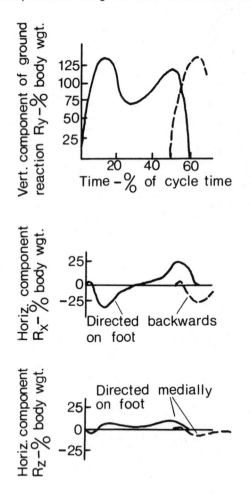

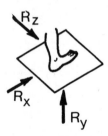

Direction of positive force components exerted by ground on foot.

Fig. 11. Typical curves of variation of ground to foot force during walking.

## Conclusion

It is probably appropriate here to present some typical data relating to the force actions which may have to be measured. Fig. 10 shows the components of ground to foot force developed during walking at normal speed on a level surface. Additional data of this type has been acquired by Harper Warlow and Clarke for different situations. It is interesting to note from these graphs that the vertifcal component of ground to foot force varies approximately between 1.3 and 0.7 x body weight during the walking cycle. The maximum value of the front to back component of force is one quarter of body weight and the maximum value of lateral force is one twentieth of body weight. Again, it is of

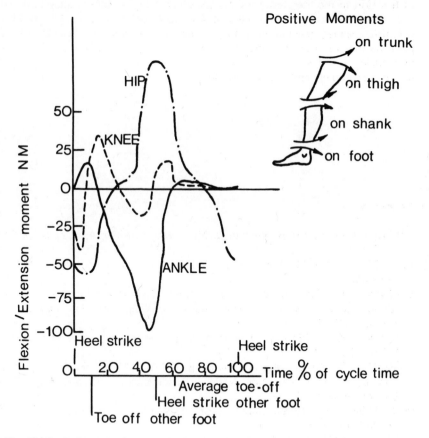

Fig. 12. *Typical curves of moment transmitted at the ankle, knee and hip of a walking individual.*

interest to note that during the period when both feet are in contact with the ground, the vertical force is maximum and the backward foot is pushing forward against the resistance of the forward foot and one foot is pushing inwards against the inward push of the other foot (Fig. 11). The effect of these load actions and the configuration of the leg is to give moment curves for the ankle, knee and hip, which are as shown in Fig. 12. These moments will be transmitted by tension in connective tissue which may be either ligamentous or connected to muscle, depending on the load action and the joint of interest. It is interesting to note that the greatest load actions occur at the ankle and at the hip, while the knee, because of the closeness of its axis to the line of action of resultant force in most situations is loaded to a much smaller degree. There exists very little information of this type in the literature for activities other than walking on a level surface and, if any readers are stimulated to investigate other types of activity in a scientific manner, making all possible relevant measurements, then the blank pages on the world of literature may usefully be filled and we can acquire more information on this complex and difficult operation, which most humans undertake routinely and without thought.

## References

AMAR, J. (1916). Trottoir dynamographique. *Compt. Rend. Acad. D. Sci.,* 163, 130-132.

CARLSOO, S. (1962). A method for studying walking on different surfaces. *Ergonomics,* 5, 271.

CUNNINGHAM, D.M. and Brown, G.W. (1952). Two devices for measuring the forces acting on the human body during walking. *Proc. Soc. Exp. Stress Analysis.* 1X, 75.

ELFTMAN, H. (1938). The measurement of the external force in walking. *Science,* 88, 152.

HARPER, F.C., Warlow, W.J. and Clarke, B.L. (1961). The forces applied to the floor by the foot in walking. National Building Studies Research Paper 32. London. HMSO:

MORRISON, J.B. (1969). Function of the knee joint in various activities. *Biomed Eng.,* 4, 573.

PAUL, J.P. (1967). Forces transmitted by joints in the human body. *Proc. Inst. Mech. Eng.,* 181, 8.

RYDELL, N.W. (1966). Forces acting on the femoral head prosthesis. *Acta Orthop. Scand. Suppl.,* 88.

SKORECKI, J. (1966). The design and construction of a new apparatus for measuring the vertical forces exerted in walking: a gait machine. *Jnl. Anal.,* 1, 429.

WHITNEY, R.J. (1957). Strength of the lifting action in man. *Ergonomics,* 1, 101.

# Author Index

# Subject Index